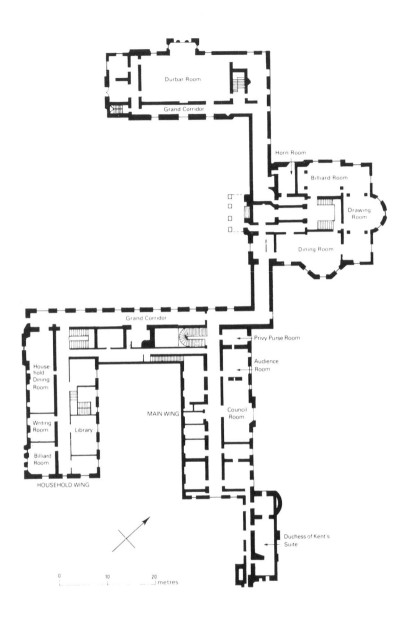

Durbar Room

Grand Corridor

Horn Room

Billiard Room

Drawing Room

Dining Room

Grand Corridor

Privy Purse Room

House hold Dining Room

Audience Room

Writing Room

Library

MAIN WING

Council Room

Billiard Room

HOUSEHOLD WING

Duchess of Kent's Suite

| 0 | 10 | 20 |
metres

*Plans of Osborne House:* Ground floor

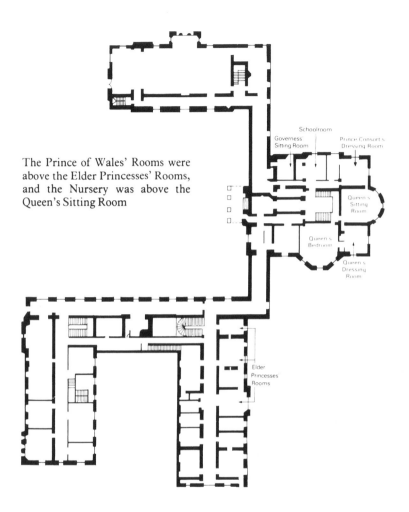

The Prince of Wales' Rooms were above the Elder Princesses' Rooms, and the Nursery was above the Queen's Sitting Room

Schoolroom

Governess Sitting Room

Prince Consort's Dressing Room

Queen's Sitting Room

Queen's Bedroom

Queen's Dressing Room

Elder Princesses Rooms

First floor

# Dear Osborne

# DEAR OSBORNE

## John Matson

*Queen Victoria's Family Life
in the Isle of Wight*

First published in Great Britain by
Hamish Hamilton Limited
90 Great Russell Street, London WC1 3PT

Copyright © by Jon A. Matson 1978

Reprinted in paperback 1981
Reprinted 1988, 1992, 1997, 2000
Reprinted 2005

British Library Cataloguing in Publication Data

Matson, John A.
Dear Osborne.
1.Osborne House, Isle of Wight – History
I. Title
942.2'82  DA664.0/

ISBN 0–241–89870–6

Printed and bound in Great Britain by Crossprint Limited
www.crossprint.co.uk

*Osborne is really too lovely. Charming and romantic and wild as Balmoral is – there is not that peaceful enjoyment that one has here of dear Osborne – the deep blue sea, myriads of brilliant flowers – the perfume of orange-blossom, magnolias, honeysuckles – roses etc. of all descriptions on the terrace, the quiet and retirement all make it a perfect paradise – which I always deeply grieve to leave.*

Queen Victoria – in a letter to
the Princess Royal, from Osborne –
July 20, 1858

*for*
*Mary*

# Contents

# List of Illustrations

The illustrations are reproduced by Gracious Permission of Her Majesty The Queen except for those on pages 18, 19, 91, 102 (above) and 147 which are reproduced by permission of the Department of the Environment. Crown copyright reserved.

# Foreword

I first became aware of the sense of history embodied in Osborne during a period of convalescence at the House during the winter of 1971 and my initial debt of gratitude must be to the then House Governor, Surgeon Captain W. J. F. Guild, R.N. (retd.) the Matron, Miss I. C. Connors, S.R.N., and the Staff of the Convalescent Home for Officers under whose care I was rapidly restored to health. I was well enough to take long walks in the grounds and soon came to appreciate what Queen Victoria had once written: '. . . It is quite a paradise', as she sat out writing under the trees.

The Queen often mentioned in her vast correspondence the murmur of the sea in the bay, the songs of birds and the sound of the fountains playing on the terraces as 'soothing to one's ears'. There is a stillness and a quality of timelessness about Osborne which is immensely restful: some said that life at Osborne was too relaxing and this might well have been true. But here at least in this home which the Queen and Prince Albert created she found peace of mind and a source of comfort to her often troubled spirit. For over seventy years since her death this solace to mind and body has been deeply appreciated by Officers from the Services and the Women's Services and, more recently, by Civil Servants, who would wish to pay tribute to all those who have inspired the old House with a new life and purpose.

In recent years over two hundred thousand people have visited Osborne annually, for it is, in its own way, unique. No other Royal home has-ever been built by, and lived in, solely by one Monarch, and in no other residence is access to the Private Apartments offered. I hope that in this book some glimpses of the way of life of the Queen and her family may awaken interest and bring closer together the years that separate us from it.

*Long Sutton, Hampshire.*
*July, 1977*

# Author's Note

Osborne is now administered by English Heritage and the King Edward VII Convalescent Home by the Civil Service Benevolent Fund. There have been some changes in the regulations and enquiries regarding admissions should be made through family doctors.

The Royal Children's quarters on the top floor of the Pavilion, until recently the House Governor's Flat, have been restored and were opened to the public in 1988.

*Farnham, Surrey*
*October, 1992*

# Acknowledgments

By gracious permission of Her Majesty The Queen I have been permitted to make use of the quotations from writings and observations by members of the Royal family referred to in the text and of certain photographs and watercolours from the Royal Collections noted in the list of illustrations, and others from the Department of the Environment, the copyright of which is vested in the Crown.

It has been a refreshing experience when embarking on a somewhat narrow field of research to discover the warmth displayed to a complete stranger. Again and again I have had only to mention my needs to encounter ready assistance and much hospitality, which have lightened both my work and my heart. I appreciate more than I can easily express the help and encouragement of the Earl Mountbatten of Burma, K.G., P.C., who, with the approval of the Broadlands Trustees, has made available for my inspection his letters from the Royal Naval College, Osborne; and the assistance of Mrs. M. Travis, Archivist at Broadlands, for her prompt attention to my enquiries. I am grateful to Sir Robin Mackworth Young, the Queen's Librarian, and to the Staff of the Royal Library, Windsor Castle, for their help and guidance, and for their criticism of the text. The responsibility for any errors remaining is entirely my own.

At Osborne House my enquiries have been aided by the kindness of the House Governor, Surgeon Captain R. S. McDonald, R.N., who has allowed me access to the House and grounds on many occasions. To Mr. E. Sibbick I owe a special debt: his knowledge of the House and its contents is probably second to none, and he has given unstintingly of his time to furnish me with facts. He has corrected many errors in the text and has patiently guided me through the intricacies of Queen Victoria's family life at Osborne. Deborah Goodenough, Head Gardener at

Osborne, kindly furnished me with both the history and the current redevelopment of the walled garden, now open to the public. I am grateful to Mr. H. H. Lambert and the Staff of the Rolls Room, at the Public Record Office, Chancery Lane, who have enabled me to delve into some of the Osborne papers. Likewise, I wish to thank Rear-Admiral P. N. Buckley, C.B., D.S.O., R. N. and his Staff at the Naval Historical Branch Library of the Admiralty. I am greatly indebted to Captain G. D. Owen, R.N. (retd.) for the opportunity of hearing at first hand his reminiscences of a Cadet's life in the early days of the Royal Naval College, and also to Mr. T. Robertson, who has furnished me with valuable information about the 'poor old swimming-bath' used by the Royal family in Osborne Bay.

Nearer home, I warmly acknowledge the assistance of Mrs. H. E. Hill, who willingly and hospitably came to my aid with the early stages of the typing; Mrs. Diana Coldicott, who generously put her library at my disposal, and whose critical but kindly appraisal enabled me to avoid some major errors and omissions; and my colleagues, C. A. N. Henderson and W. L. Fryer, who read the script and made some valuable suggestions. The Staff of the Fleet and Farnham Public Libraries have been particularly helpful in tracking down elusive books required for reference.

I particularly wish to thank members of the Department of the Environment in London: Mr. Peter Curnow, who encouraged my venture and authorised my access to certain illustrations; Mrs. Susan Hannabuss, who dealt with my enquiries and ferreted out elusive information for me; and Mrs. Mary Harper, of the Photographic Library, who not only provided the material I required but also anticipated my needs.

I owe to my old friend, Mark Baker, a long-lasting and personal debt which he will modestly disclaim but which I gratefully acknowledge. Finally, to my family, who have uncomplainingly borne my preoccupation with this work, my very grateful thanks.

I am indebted to the following publishers for permission to make use of extracts from the works indicated in the References:-

To Macmillan, London and Basingstoke: *Dear and Honoured Lady* by Hope Dyson and Charles Tennyson; *Henry Ponsonby: His Life from his Letters* by Arthur Ponsonby; *Thomas Cubitt, Master Builder* by Hermione Hobhouse.

To John Murray (Publishers) Ltd.: *Life with Queen Victoria* by Victor Mallet; *The Queen Thanks Sir Howard* by M. H. McClintock; *Correspondence of Sarah Spencer, Lady Lyttelton* ed. Mrs. Wyndham.

To Evans Brothers Ltd.: *Dearest Child, Dearest Mama, Your Dear Letter* ed. Roger Fulford; *The Shy Princess* by David Duff; *My Memories of Six Reigns* by H.H. Princess Marie Louise.

To Hamish Hamilton Ltd.: *Queen Victoria: Her Life and Times* copyright © 1972 by Cecil Woodham-Smith.

To James Nisbet & Co.: *Twenty Years at Court* by the Hon. Eleanor Stanley.

To Curtis Brown Ltd.: *Lady Lytton's Court Diary* ed. Mary Lutyens.

To The Cornhill Magazine: *The Diaries of F. W. Gibbs.*

*The Illustrated London News.*

To Weidenfeld & Nicolson: *Victoria, R.I.* by Elizabeth Longford.

# Introduction: The Osborne Scene

At the western end of Spithead, the famous anchorage which extends from Portsmouth to Cowes, the two grey Italianate towers which mark Osborne rise above the wooded hills of the Isle of Wight. At the far end of the central valley stands the long stucco building, with its green and white canopy shading Queen Victoria's private sitting-room, and there is a glimpse of tall windows and terraces. The valley descends to the sandy shore of Osborne Bay beside which stand the landing pier house, also in the Italian style, and the tiny pavilion where the Queen often sat watching her children and grandchildren at play on the beach. The landing-stage and the pier have vanished; only the stumps of their supports lie embedded in the sand. Over the long years the sea has eroded the shoreline; much of the Queen's Drive has now disintegrated and trees have toppled into the water to lie rotting on the seam of blue clay which emerges on the flanks of the bay. Down here by the sea some of the gravel pathways are overgrown and their tracks are all but obliterated.

The death of Queen Victoria at Osborne in 1901 is for many the sum of their knowledge of this unique, once-Royal property. Its function for over half a century as one of the more informal Royal homes remains largely neglected: few outside the Wardrooms of the Royal Navy remember that for nearly twenty years a Naval College flourished here – when the grounds which had once been dominated by a magnificent, lonely figure echoed with shouts of command, bugle calls and the laughter and clear voices of boys. Later, the Cadets went away and the buildings which had housed them were demolished or put to other uses, and Osborne regained its silence. It had also been used during

*Prince Alfred, Mr. F. W. Gibbs, the Prince of Wales. 1854.*
(Photo. Fenton)

*The Royal Nursery 1873*

this period as a Convalescent Home for Officers, and indeed, so it is today, a place where members of the Services can find refreshment from its peace and beauty. In 1954 the Queen consented to the opening of the Private Apartments to the public, and every summer many thousands avail themselves of the opportunity, unique as it is, of seeing this example of Royal and Victorian domesticity.

There is a great poignancy about Osborne such as there is in few other English homes. Its history is comparatively recent but, in its own way, eventful; yet so much is known of those spacious days that, as we look upon the miniature garden tools of the Royal children down by the Swiss Cottage, or linger in the Prince Consort's study, seeing his walking sticks in their stand by the door, we can almost effortlessly recreate life at Osborne a hundred years ago.

Inevitably, we ask ourselves many questions as we move through the house: what manner of woman was Queen Victoria, who gave her name to a whole age of English history; what did she do here, and how did she order her life and the lives of those around her; what family life did she have; and then, when she had gone, when her coffin had been carried out through the front door on her last journey to Windsor and the Mausoleum at Frogmore, what happened to bring a long line of convalescent officers and a throng of Naval Cadets into these quiet precincts? Some of the answers are to be found here, in memories and scenes bringing life and meaning to Osborne, which is part of our heritage.

# The Children of Queen Victoria and Prince Albert

**1 Princess Victoria** ('Vicky')

b. 1840 — Princess Royal.

m. 1858 — Prince Frederick William of Prussia; later Crown Princess of Prussia and Empress Frederick of Germany.
8 children; the eldest became Kaiser Wilhelm II.

d. 1901

**2 Prince Albert Edward** ('Bertie')

b. 1841 — Prince of Wales

m. 1863 — Princess Alexandra of Denmark
5 children: Prince Albert Victor – d. 1892; Prince George m. Princess May of Teck later King George V. d. 1936 3 daughters.

1901 — Acceded as King Edward VII.
d. 1910

**3 Princess Alice**

b. 1843
m. 1862 — Grand Duke of Hesse-Darmstadt
2 sons, 5 daughters.

d. 1878

**4 Prince Alfred** ('Affie')

b. 1844 — Duke of Edinburgh
m. 1874 — Princess Marie of Russia
1 son, 4 daughters.

d. 1900

**5 Princess Helena** ('Lenchen')

b. 1846
m. 1866 — Prince Christian of Schleswig-Holstein
4 children: Prince Christian Victor 1867–1900, Prince Albert, Princess Helena Victoria, Princess Marie Louise (d. 1957)

d. 1923

**6 Princess Louise**

b. 1848
m. 1871 — The Marquess of Lorne, later Duke of Argyll
No issue

d. 1939

| 7 **Prince Arthur** | b. 1850 | Duke of Connaught |
| | m. 1879 | Louise, Princess of Prussia |
| | | 1 son, 2 daughters. |
| | d. 1942 | |

| 8 **Prince Leopold** | b. 1853 | Duke of Albany |
| | m. 1882 | Helena, Princess of Waldeck-Pyrmont |
| | | 1 son, 1 daughter. |
| | d. 1884 | (*Haemophilia*) |

| 9 **Princess Beatrice** | b. 1857 | |
| | m. 1885 | Prince Henry of Battenberg |
| | | 3 sons, 1 daughter. |
| | d. 1944 | |

*Part One*

1843–1901

# Beginnings

Osborne House, the home of Lady Isabella Blachford, was '. . . a handsome, square edifice, seated at the head of an ample lawn, which slopes gently to a valley open to a sea beach. The whole park, strictly private, extends down to the sea, with good landing places . . .'[1] The estate comprised several hundred acres in which roamed a large herd of deer. It was situated on high ground a mile outside East Cowes, and from its windows a sweeping panorama of Spithead and the Solent as far as Portsmouth could be obtained. It was not remote, yet it afforded some seclusion and, of course, it was not far from London. Small wonder then that it should appeal to a young family of considerable means, who were for ever in the public eye, and who must remain accessible to those in power.

In 1843 Queen Victoria's domestic life was hardly enviable. By this time Princess Victoria, Prince Albert Edward and Princess Alice had been born and, with the possible exception of Windsor Castle, there was no Royal residence really suitable for the Queen and her family. Buckingham Palace, which already had been rebuilt at vast public expense, overlooked to the south a large area of squalid tenements, and there was no room for the children, nor any likelihood of Parliamentary approval being granted for the provision of more accommodation. The Royal nurseries were to be found among the attics of the North Wing. There remained Brighton Pavilion, the private fantasy of the former Prince Regent. Once, it might almost have been suitable, but by this time the surrounding areas had been developed and the Royal windows afforded no view of the sea, whilst the growing popularity of Brighton itself as a watering-place brought crowds which milled about the Queen as though she were some kind of raree-show. There the situation had become intolerable, and the Queen realised that she could never use the Pavilion again.

Things were really no better at Windsor. Although there was more space the public had access almost to the doors of the Castle and movement outside the building became virtually impossible. But the public image of the Monarchy had improved, and the sometimes ribald hostility which had greeted King George IV was being replaced by a steadily increasing respect for the tiny, (she was only five feet tall) dignified woman who was Queen of Great Britain and of a rapidly growing Empire. Royalty was now synonymous with respectability – though there still lurked a number of somewhat sinister, raffish uncles – and a measure of isolation was desirable. The Queen's longing for a home of her own was intensified by visits to France and a cruise along the South Coast. The germ of an idea was born. On 19 October, 1843, the Queen wrote: 'During our usual morning walk Albert and I talked about buying a place of our own, which would be so nice; perhaps Norris Castle might be something to think of.'[2]

Almost inevitably the Queen's thoughts had turned to the Isle of Wight. In 1831 the Duchess of Kent, Victoria's mother, had taken her to Norris Castle, a stately, rambling building actually adjacent to the Osborne estate, for a summer holiday. In 1833 the Princess and her mother again visited the Island during one of those tours which her uncle, King William IV, so cordially detested. They again stayed at Norris Castle and the Princess extended her acquaintance with the Island which afterwards was to become so closely associated with her. She explored Whippingham Church and East Cowes; she toured Nelson's 'Victory', then afloat at Portsmouth, and moved westwards by stages. She was only fourteen and the happiness she found in the Isle of Wight remained in her memory.

During the early years of the Queen's reign she and Prince Albert spent less and less time at Buckingham Palace, residing for the greater part at Windsor. For one thing, the Prince was unused to city life and, being a serious-minded young man, was swiftly disenchanted with the great urban sprawl, even then being developed with astonishing rapidity by men like Thomas Cubitt, and he did not care for the frivolity of London society. The Queen, more susceptible to its delights but quite ready to conform to the Prince's notions of happiness and rejoicing in her

*The original Osborne House c. 1844. Watercolour by C. R. Stanley*

role of the submissive wife, soon came to believe that peace and quiet were only to be secured away from the capital: '. . . the extreme weight and thickness of the atmosphere' injured her health – we must not forget the 'pea-soup' fogs of the cities, which later were to be so vividly described by Dickens, and in consequence her visits to London became even more infrequent. She began to make enquiries about a place in the country: in 1843 she revisited Norris Castle and wished she had been able to afford it when it came on the market, and before Christmas negotiations, guided by Sir Robert Peel, the Prime Minister, were in hand to take Osborne on lease, with an option to purchase. Prince Albert made a flying visit of inspection in March, and the Queen herself arrived in August, 1844, after the birth of her fourth child, Prince Alfred. She wrote, somewhat optimistically, as it turned out: 'I am delighted with the house over all which we went, and which is so complete and snug. The rooms are small, look very nice, and the offices and stabling very good. With some alterations for the children it might be made an excellent house.'[3]

Sir Robert Peel advocated caution. He was ever mindful of the effect on the public of expenditure on Royal residences. In reply,

## The Principal Descendants of

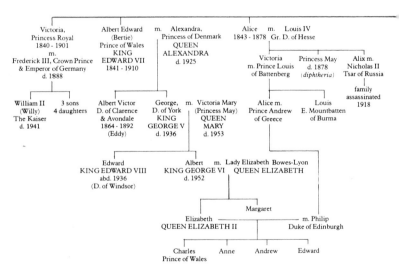

QUEEN VICTORIA
1819 - 1901

Victoria, Princess Royal 1840 - 1901 m. Frederick III, Crown Prince & Emperor of Germany d. 1888

Albert Edward (Bertie) Prince of Wales KING EDWARD VII 1841 - 1910 m. Alexandra, Princess of Denmark QUEEN ALEXANDRA d. 1925

Alice m. Louis IV 1843 - 1878 Gr. D. of Hesse

Victoria m. Prince Louis of Battenberg

Princess May d. 1878 (diphtheria)

Alix m. Nicholas II Tsar of Russia

family assassinated 1918

William II (Willy) The Kaiser d. 1941

3 sons 4 daughters

Albert Victor D. of Clarence & Avondale 1864 - 1892 (Eddy)

George, D. of York KING GEORGE V d. 1936 m. Victoria Mary (Princess May) QUEEN MARY d. 1953

Alice m. Prince Andrew of Greece

Louis E. Mountbatten of Burma

Edward KING EDWARD VIII abd. 1936 (D. of Windsor)

Albert KING GEORGE VI d. 1952 m. Lady Elizabeth Bowes-Lyon QUEEN ELIZABETH

Margaret

Elizabeth QUEEN ELIZABETH II m. Philip Duke of Edinburgh

Charles Prince of Wales

Anne

Andrew

Edward

Prince Albert pointed out the advantages that the purchase would bring: neglected agricultural land could be made profitable, new plantations laid out, its healthy situation and proximity to the Navy at Portsmouth. Finally he mentioned the Queen's desire to have her own private property, which he urged was 'so reasonable, and the accomplishment of it will be such a source of amusement, comfort and satisfaction to her, myself and her family, that I think it ought to be fulfilled.'[4]

In the Prince's opinion the house could be made quite adequate by new kitchens for which there was a very good site in an open yard near the present offices, a dormitory for the servants over the stables (!), in fact, 'only the addition of a few rooms to make it into a very suitable and comfortable residence for the Queen and children and part of the Suite.'[5]

This, though, was the view of the optimistic house-buyer, who sees all through rose-coloured spectacles and, once past a certain point of hesitation, is not to be deterred by defects or the objections of others less partial in their views. *The Illustrated London News*, however, was more realistic in its description of the house: 'The mansion has on the ground floor a drawing-room, dining-room and library with two ante-rooms and halls. The first and

# Queen Victoria and Prince Albert

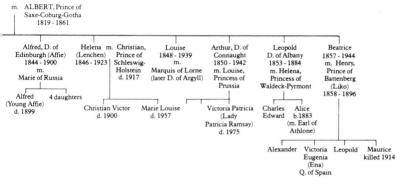

second floors contain sixteen bed and dressing-rooms; very inadequate for a royal suite.'[6]

Yes, indeed, but *The Illustrated London News* could hardly have kept up with the wealth of ideas which began to flow during that first idyllic visit. The Queen was convinced that the house was exactly what she wanted, and negotiations continued. After a price of £28,000 had been agreed Lady Isabella demanded £30,000. The Queen and Prince Albert then offered £26,000 without furniture or crops, which was apparently accepted.

A few weeks later Mr. Anson, the Prince's private secretary, reported that Lady Isabella was behaving 'very ill'. She insisted that she was entitled to the fixtures and would rather abandon the whole contract than give way. She considered that she had been ill-used by the Queen because her furniture had not been taken at a valuation.[6a] On the other hand, she might deserve a measure of sympathy; the Queen's agents were perfectly capable of driving a hard bargain. A contract had actually been signed by her, which could have been enforced, though this would not have been desirable. Finally, after Sir James Clark, the Queen's Physician, had visited the locality to check the wholesome properties of the air, Osborne came into Royal hands in May, 1845. So sure had everyone been of satisfactorily completing the sale, that during the previous January plans for improving the house had been drawn up. Mr. Anson, who lived in a Cubitt house in Eaton Place, wrote to Edward White, the Queen's agent: 'One of the most Eminent Builders in London has been employed by Her Majesty to survey the house at Osborne, and has reported that it could not be converted by mere alterations and repairs into a Residence affording even that modest degree of accommodation . . . but that the construction of a new house is indispensably necessary, and would be less expensive in the end than the repair of the present.'[7]

On the completion of the sale the Queen and Prince Albert made a two-day visit to Osborne. Thomas Cubitt was sent for, and he and the Prince discussed the building plan as well as urgent repairs and alterations to the existing house, which were to be put in hand at once. At last the Queen could tell her Uncle Leopold: 'You will, I am sure, be pleased to hear that we have succeeded in purchasing Osborne, in the Isle of Wight . . . It sounds so snug and nice to have a place of *one's own*, quiet and retired, and free from all Woods and Forests, and other charming Departments who really are the plague of one's life.'[8]

This last remark was a tilt at those Government Departments whose responsibility it was to maintain the Royal residences, and against whose anachronisms the Prince had already come into real conflict in his endeavours to eliminate inefficiency and out-moded tradition. It was, for example, the work of one Depart-ment to clean the outside of the Palace windows and of another to clean the inside, with the result that the two sides were never clean together, making the fogs seem even worse than they were. The Royal decision to employ Cubitt was the logical result of a great longing for independence. Edward Blore and Sir Charles Barry, and other leading architects of the day, already had con-nections with 'Woods and Forests', and although Blore was invited to prepare a design for the alterations at Osborne, nothing came of it. Cubitt, on the other hand, was one of the foremost men of his time, occupying a unique position, and having at his command unparalleled resources in the building world: his own draughtsmen, masons, workshops and forges. Furthermore, he could be relied upon to work to a fixed price and to within a given time.

The decision was a happy one. As we shall see, Cubitt did far more than merely build Osborne, though that in itself would have been no small undertaking. Prince Albert was a man of ideas and intellect, and we may assume that the house in its pres-ent form was a blend of the Cubitt style – a square, strong struc-ture embodying the use of innovations like cast-iron girders instead of wooden beams, insulation of a layer of sea shells be-tween floors, cement and stucco – and of a certain breadth of vision on the Prince's part. Whether or not the view from Osborne of the long reach of Spithead really reminded the Prince of the Bay of Naples, there is more than a touch of the Italianate, not only on the exterior with its twin campaniles, alcoves and ter-races, but also in the tiled floor of the Corridor, with 'Salve' inset by the door, and the plethora of marble busts in their niches. Osborne was his version of an Italian villa, blended with Cubitt's solidity; the gardens that reach down to the central valley are adorned with fountains and bronze statues in the Renaissance manner; and he certainly achieved his aim in the semi-circular arches of the balconies and in the shallow, pantiled roofs of the towers which form so conspicuous a feature of Osborne. The

Prince was a man who enjoyed making plans, and going into things deeply, so it is likely that he and Cubitt worked out rough sketches together, initially perhaps in the old house, and thus formed the basis for the finished plans to be drawn up by Cubitt's men.

It was a period of great happiness for the Prince, whose natural abilities and enthusiasms, previously checked by many a snub from the 'charming Departments', were given full scope in those early days. In May, 1845, another visit was made, and on the 12th the Queen wrote: 'It does my heart good to see how my beloved Albert enjoys it all, and is so full of admiration of the place, and of all the plans and improvements he means to carry out. He is hardly to be kept at home for a moment.'[9]

On this visit she herself saw Cubitt and discussed the alterations, and the Prince then 'settled with him about the new house and the alterations and improvements to the old'.[10] The preliminary work proceeded apace; plans and specifications were drawn up which formed 'the contract between the Queen and Mr. Cubitt.' On June 23 the Queen recorded in her Journal: 'Soon after breakfast the laying of the foundation stone of the new house took place. A way was arranged for us to the foundation and Albert and I with the two eldest children went down. First of all a small glass box containing coins of my realm and an inscription recording who was present was placed in a hole in the ground and cemented over, which we and the children carried out. The large foundation stone was placed over it and we all went round and hammered on it.'[11] For any family it would have been a memorable and enjoyable occasion.

Work progressed rapidly once the footings were in: by the end of September the house was up, but not roofed, and on 1 March, 1846, Cubitt escorted the Queen and the Prince on a tour of the building. 'The staircase and ceiling are in!' exclaimed the Queen rapturously, 'and it will be quite delightful. I can hardly believe we shall be living in this charming house, built by ourselves in a few months.'[12] Whenever possible the Royal couple came down, viewing and approving all they saw. The hall was not large and intimidating, and was little more than a staircase well; if not exactly 'domestic' it must have seemed so after the grandeur of the Royal palaces; the rooms were small and few in number – too few, it soon appeared, and the main wing rose like a phoenix from the ruins of the old house, cleverly incorporating part of the

*Osborne: Construction of the Terrace 1847. Watercolour by W. L. Leitch*

offices and retaining part of the walls of an even earlier Osborne House, built in the seventeenth century.

Before the move into the new Pavilion wing, the Queen held a Privy Council in the old house, which was attended by Charles Greville, that sardonic commentator on Royal and national affairs. He found the trip from London – special train to Gosport in $2\frac{1}{4}$ hours and Black Eagle steamer to East Cowes – 'very agreeable' – but Osborne itself was 'a miserable place and such a vile house that the Lords of the Council had no place to remain in but the Entrance Hall, so we walked about looking at the new house the Queen is building; it is very ugly and the whole concern wretched enough. They will spend first and last a great deal of money there, but it is her own money and not the nation's.'[13]

The move to the newly completed Pavilion was accomplished. On 15 September, 1846, Lady Lyttelton, Lady Superintendent of the Royal Children, wrote: 'Nobody caught cold or smelt paint . . . Everything in the house is quite new, and the dining room looked very handsome. The windows lighted by the brilliant lamps in the room must have been seen far out at sea. After dinner we all rose to drink the Queen's and Prince's health as a *housewarming*, and after it the Prince said, very naturally and simply but sincerely, "We have a hymn" (he called it a psalm) "in Germany for such occasions. It begins" – and then he quoted two lines in German which I could not quote right meaning a prayer to bless our going out and coming in. It was dry and quaint, being Luther's; but we all perceived that he was feeling it. . . . And truly entering a new house, a new palace, is a solemn thing to do.'[14]

Even in these first days in their new and private home that unique quality which belongs only to Osborne had begun to develop. For one thing, the owners were young – not yet thirty, and the proud parents of five healthy children. They were well off, and were already contemplating additions to the estate, which was eventually to grow to over two thousand acres. They were domesticated, in love, and generally, happy. But they could never entirely escape from the pressures of Royal duty; the despatch boxes as we shall see later arrived from the seat of government in a steady procession, and cast an inexorable burden upon the Queen and, increasingly, upon the Prince.

The Queen herself had a great longing, which was seldom

achieved, to be 'snug', 'comfortable' and 'cosy'. Into these words may be read a degree of 'ordinariness' in the character of Queen Victoria, and we may well understand her regret that the 'dear little house' which she had bought at Osborne, had to be demolished. It was sad, but inevitable. It was perhaps out of sentiment that Cubitt rescued the porch of the early house and set it into the wall on the far side of the lawn from the portico of the new house. It would remind the Queen of those early days in the Isle of Wight, and of her first goings out and comings in.

Meanwhile, the building continued: the Household Wing was completed and, soon afterwards, the Main Wing which was joined to the Pavilion by arcades on the first two floors – though the upper passageway was not protected from the weather for some years, the Queen herself being almost impervious to cold and unable to understand the susceptibility of others. There was a Council Chamber, not large, but ornate, several small rooms for Audiences, and a suite for the Duchess of Kent. In the second, parallel wing built for the Household the courtiers had their rooms, dined and relaxed in a billiard room where smoking was allowed.

Alterations were made to the servants' quarters and to the stabling as requirements dictated, but Cubitt's men were unobtrusive and the greater part of the work was carried out in the absence of the Royal family, who came down shortly before moving in. Lady Lyttelton wrote:

> *Osborne, August 18, 1846.*
> Yesterday walking home I was seized with admiration for the weather and the scene . . . Patches of children, each attended by their scarlet footmen, shining in the distance – Mr. Anson escorting Lady Jocelyn with her two babies across the park. The Prince very busy with builders. The Equerries charging about – all looked rather interesting and Royal . . .[15]

On August 26 Lady Lyttelton continued: '. . . I have been out on a pleasant stroll about the brick and mortar heaps, and then into the lower garden, and there I saw the children burst out of the house after tea in great joy . . .'[16] Shortly afterwards the Royal family went on a cruise to Cornwall and the Channel Islands which proved a great success, though Lady Lyttelton deplored the lack of routine in her charges' lives.

Even in his absence Prince Albert's guiding hand was everywhere – and he was a good employer. On August 9 the Superintendent of the Royal Children had written:

It is pleasant to see how earnestly Prince Albert tries to do
the best about this place, giving work to as many labourers as
possible, but not making any haste, so as to make it last, and
keep at a steady useful pitch, not to over-excite the market.
His bailiff (I mean, of course, the Queen's) has dismissed
quantities of men lately, because it is harvest time, that they
may work for others, telling them all, that the moment any
man is out of employment, that he is to come back here, and
will, without fail, find work to do. This is doing good very
wisely.[17]

He continued to do very wisely. Work at Osborne extended
into the fifties, providing steady employment; and the final additions – the Victoria Hall, at first the Orangery, then used as a
chapel, and the Durbar Room, were not completed until long
after his death. There was also a steady growth in the number of
workers on the estate as more land was purchased needing cultivation and maintenance; and the whole area was opened up by
nearly twenty miles of walks and drives. Osborne was easily
accessible from London and Windsor, and provided the Prince
with a constant outlet for his active brain.

The Queen herself found in Osborne all that she had hoped
for, and more. The Hon. Eleanor Stanley, a Maid of Honour,
wrote on 27 July, 1848:

The whole Royal family, children, Queen and all seem to
be out the whole day long;
I don't believe the Queen thinks of reading a despatch or
doing anything in the way of business, further than scrib-
bling her name where it is required while she is here, and she
told Lady Canning "she had not read out of a book since
February". She draws a good deal, and walks about and
enjoys herself. The children dine and tea in the garden, and
run about to their hearts' content.[18]

The holiday atmosphere continued, despite the problems
over the Prince of Wales' education and the domestic troubles

inevitable in so large a family. Eight years later Miss Stanley wrote:

> After lunch I took the Prussian ladies to the seashore where they looked for shells . . . The Queen arrived about 6.30 from Aldershot with the rest of the Royal party and I had to go out immediately with the Princesses to their garden to eat gooseberries and strawberries – at least the few the squirrels had left – and see how everything was getting on.[19] There were more walks to the Swiss Cottage and to the farm, and drives all over the Island; and cruises in the *Fairy*. During one such trip – a voyage up Southampton Water to Netley Hospital – tea was served on board: '. . . presided over by the Queen, on the deck of the *Fairy*; our tablecloth well lashed to the legs of the table, otherwise our fine silver teapots and all our grandeur just as if we were at home.'[20]

Evenings with the Queen were often spent quietly with much of the entertainment being provided by the Royal family and the Household. How well we can picture the Drawing-Room scene in March, 1861, described by Miss Stanley:

> In the evening we had music – that is, I played, and the Queen turned over the pages; the Prince praised, and Princess Alice criticised me; after which we ladies adjourned to the Queen's round table and worked till 11, while the Prince and some of the gentlemen played at billiards and the rest at whist . . .[21]

Such was the family life at Osborne in those halcyon days before the Prince's death cut off the light and happiness like the descending of a curtain, leaving the Queen grief-stricken and numb with loneliness and despair.

# Prince Albert

Prince Albert of Saxe-Coburg-Gotha, Queen Victoria's husband – and first cousin – was very much a man of his time; deeply interested in the sciences, systematic, logical, efficient. The Royal marriage was not popular in England; the Prince was everywhere received dutifully but without enthusiasm, and there were those in high places who feared that this young German would exercise an undue influence over their Sovereign. The young couple were very different in temperament: the Queen was vivacious and active, and enjoyed the gaiety and glitter of London life: the Prince was serious, painstaking and conscientious to a degree. He was ambitious not for himself but for the Crown. His reforms, however, brought him enemies: those that he carried out in the Royal palaces were bitterly resented by the officials who stood to lose by them. For instance, the Prince learned that the candles were replaced daily in all the rooms, whether or not they had been used: the 'perks' were enormous. For Prince Albert work, duty and thoroughness were spelt with capital letters, and remorselessly he drove himself harder and harder, ultimately to his death. In a letter to his daughter, his beloved 'Vicky', he wrote:

*Osborne, 23rd May, 1859.*
Your letter of the 20th found me in the enjoyment of the most glorious air, the most fragrant odours, the merriest choirs of birds, and the most luxuriant verdure; and were there not so many things that reminded one of the so-called world (that is, of miserable men), one might give oneself up wholly to the enjoyment of the real world. There is no such good fortune, however, for poor me; and, this being so, one's feelings remain under the influence of the treadmill of never-ending business. The donkey in Carisbrooke, which you will remember, is my

true counterpart. He, too, would rather munch thistles in the Castle Moat, than turn round in the wheel at the Castle Well; and small are the thanks he gets for his labours.[1]

Always there was work and more work. As his abilities came to be recognised and his special role within the Monarchy to be accepted, his genius for organisation was much in demand, and the volume of work entrusted to him increased sharply. He was promoted from 'Blotter of the Queen's Letters' to the valued author of drafts and memoranda, and the Queen, realising his flair for the very work in which she felt least able to interest herself, gratefully leaned ever more heavily upon him. As the father of nine children, a grandfather before his death, and married to the Queen for over twenty years, he has come to be thought of as an aging, patriarchal figure; in fact he died, prematurely balding, a sick, tired man, at the early age of forty-two. It is a tribute befitting Prince Albert's abilities that his last draft, written a fortnight before his death, concerned the 'Trent' affair, when a British ship was boarded by a party of Americans, and was acclaimed a masterpiece of diplomacy which would go far to prevent a serious deterioration in Anglo-American relations.

In effect Prince Albert became the Queen's private and personal secretary: he read – and understood – despatches, often preparing for his wife a simplified and abbreviated version which always contained the kernel of the matter. He drafted documents for her approval; he laid foundation stones by the dozen, opened Institutions and presided over Royal Commissions at a time when the growth of technology was accelerating rapidly and needed the guiding but impartial hand of a gifted man, and wrote his inaugural speeches himself.

Albert was intensely nervous before such occasions; he was 'tortured by the prospect', could barely eat, and his digestion was impaired, yet he was received with respect and genuine applause. After his Presidential Address to the British Association for the Advancement of Science he was given a standing ovation from some of the most learned men in the land. He chaired committees and it was soon found that once he had undertaken a cause, he could be guaranteed not only to see it through to its completion, but also to look into every aspect of its foundation and development with care. He was President of the Royal Commission administering the Fund raised by the nation in memory

*Kitchen and Offices, Osborne House 1867. Food was taken to the Pavilion Wing and the Household Dining Room on trolleys, the dishes being surrounded by hotwater containers. Photo by Disderi*

of the great Duke of Wellington, who died in 1852. It was to be used to found a College whose special aim was to educate the sons of deceased officers. He was not a chairman in name only: his interests led him into practical details. He had many suggestions for the design of the College buildings, which today bear a faint resemblance to the Palace of Versailles, and wrote a detailed memorandum on behalf of the Queen, instituting the annual award of a medal to an outstanding scholar. Similarly, his enquiring mind led him to consider aspects of training, with special reference to conduct, of officer cadets at Sandhurst. For them, and for the schoolboys of Wellington, he provided a library of books for their studies.

So it was at Osborne. For the Prince the work there came as a change, a greater domesticity, but no less work. After the wing

for the Household was completed came the building of the terraces with their massive retaining walls. In 1851 the central valley was remodelled; its rough, uneven slopes were graded, the Italian Walk was made, and trees and ornamental shrubs were planted. On March 25 the Royal family returned to London busy with plans for the opening of the Exhibition in Hyde Park, which was the Prince's brain-child and particular triumph. Meanwhile, the firm of Cubitt worked on, repairing and building cottages, constructing the water-tank on the Mount to supply the fountains, and installing an ice-house, invaluable in those days before refrigeration.

Even the comparative seclusion of Osborne furnished the Prince with examples of the technological progress of the age. In 1853 there was a Naval Review at Spithead, which the Queen and the Prince attended. In a letter to Baron Stockmar, his old friend and adviser, he wrote: 'The gigantic ships . . . went, without sails, and propelled only by the screw, *eleven miles an hour*, & this against wind and tide.'[2] There was a still deeper significance in this event, and in a military Review held at Chobham in the same year, which the couple also attended. We were, as a nation, unprepared against the threat of aggression, and these reviews were '. . . the evidence of the Prince's persistent representations to the Government in recent years. A programme of, at least comparative, modernisation was under way.' It was none too soon, for already the Crimean War was threatening.

It was at Osborne, too, that Prince Albert had another opportunity to express his interest in scientific affairs, this time by the arrival at East Cowes of the *Resolute*. This ship had carried an expedition to the Arctic in 1854 and had been abandoned in the ice. She had been found by American explorers, freed and taken to America for refitting. She was then returned to England by Congress as a present to the Queen. On the *Resolute*'s arrival at Cowes, the Queen and the Prince came down personally to accept her. In 1965 the bell of the *Resolute* was returned to the United States by the Prime Minister, as a gift from the people of Britain.

A final instance of the Prince's wide interests may be given. He was an early and enthusiastic conservationist. It was at Osborne that he had an opportunity to experiment with the processing of raw sewage for re-cycling and subsequent use in agriculture. With the assistance of Mr. Lyon Playfair he was to perfect this, and he applied the process successfully on the estate. As usual, he saw in the scheme a wider implication: 'This has become for England an important public question. All previous plans would have cost millions, mine costs next to nothing.' (Letter to Baron Stockmar, 1850). In the result it worked at Osborne where the ground fell steeply, but on level land it was found to be impracticable.

Always in the Prince the serious side of his nature predominated, though he could be light-hearted in conversation. He was often by no means clever with his wife and family – his own childhood had not equipped him to mediate gently when disharmony occurred. At times there were hysterical outbursts and recriminations from the Queen: the Prince failed signally to cope: he would write her a memorandum on the subject, as he did in

1859: 'You have again lost your self-control, quite unnecessarily.
I did not say a word which could wound you, and I did not begin
the conversation, but you had followed me about and continued
it from room to room . . . I do my duty towards you even though
it means that life is embittered by "scenes" when it should be
governed by love and harmony . . . You hurt me desperately and
at the same time do not help yourself.'[3]

The Prince was stoic in face of the criticism which he encountered, but he was sensitive to it; his constitution was not strong
and for several years before his death he was more or less chroni-
cally afflicted with catarrh, rheumatism and dyspepsia; a morbid
depression settled on him, and he ceased to cling to life. The
Queen was aware that he was over-working but she resented the
fact that it interfered with their relationship more than because
it was affecting his health. This was never more true than after
the death of her mother when she suffered a nervous breakdown.

So much for the man who stood beside Cubitt and watched
Osborne grow, who placed the shrubberies and laid out plantations, and helped to tend them with his own hands. The Prince
loved gardening, which he saw as a creative exercise: '. . . In this
the artist who lays out the work and devises a garment for a piece
of ground has the delight of seeing his work live and grow hour
by hour; and, while it is growing, he is able to polish, to cut and
carve, to fill up here and there, to hope, and to love.'[4] Even while
the wings of the House were under construction the Prince
turned his attention to the walled garden near the Prince of Wales
entrance. This had been in existence in some form since the 18th
Century and was referred to as "the Kitchen Garden". The
Queen took a keen interest in the progress: on 22 June 1846 she
recorded in her Journal: "Went with Albert to the Kitchen
Garden, which is in great beauty & full of pinks, & fruit trees, all
covered with fruit. A great many fine plants Albert bought are also
there." By 1849 the Prince had refurbished it to become largely
devoted to fruit and flowers, since the vegetables for the house
were largely supplied from the gardens at Frogmore.

In the same year he wrote to Baron Stockmar quite cheerfully:
'I am very well, all but my stomach, which is decidedly *not*
better.'[5] And a few days later to Vicky: 'I am overwhelmed with
papers, and can scarcely wrestle through them; therefore, even
to you, I must say farewell so soon.'[6]

A fortnight later, just before the family left Osborne for

Christmas at Windsor, he again wrote to Vicky: 'We have had a fall of nine inches of snow, which looked wonderfully beautiful. I have all but broken my arms against the trees and shrubs, in clearing them, with poles, of the snow, which would otherwise have wholly crushed the fine evergreens and threatened to make havoc of the cypresses especially '[7]

We come here to a strange anomaly in the Prince's character. For so artistic a man he was singularly insensitive at times; for him the architecture of nature – the design of a garden or a wood, the ordering of an efficient estate – was a creative achievement, yet at Coburg he once participated in a slaughter of deer with seeming indifference, rounding them up into enclosures and shooting them at close range – he was not a good shot. This exploit did not endear the Prince to the English public; there was an outcry against such unsporting behaviour. He then confined his activities to stalking at Balmoral and the occasional pheasant shoot at Osborne. The Queen, who used to follow the guns, quickly learned not to enquire too closely about his own 'bag'.

The wild, mountainous country around Balmoral, which more nearly resembled that of his homeland, did more for the Prince's health than the mild relaxing air of Osborne, which nevertheless soothed his tired spirit. Beyond the windows of the Queen's sitting-room is a stone balcony on which, in the summer evenings, the Royal parents stood to listen to the song of the nightingales. Of all bird-songs Prince Albert loved these the best, 'listening for them in the happy, peaceful walks he used to take with the Queen in the woods, and whistling to them in their own peculiar long note, which they invariably answer! or standing out there at night to hear their song.' Once a policeman patrolling the grounds at night discovered a man standing silently by some trees; when detained, he made no answer but accompanied him back to the house, where in the light of oil-lamps, the constable was greatly disconcerted to learn that he had arrested the Prince.

Osborne was too near the Capital for complete seclusion: times were often difficult and anxious, but a peaceful spirit was to be found there and the Prince loved his creation and derived from it a fascinating and lasting hobby.

## The Children of Osborne

In everything connected with Queen Victoria's life the time-scale is impressive. The nursery days of Princess Beatrice overlapped the marriage of her eldest sister, the Princess Royal. For twenty years and more the voices of the Queen's infant children were raised in tears and laughter and the period from 1845 to 1861 was among the busiest and happiest that Osborne was ever to know: it was followed by as long an interval of sombreness, when the shadow of Prince Albert's death fell most heavily on the Queen.

*Queen Victoria's Letter-heading, Osborne, c. 1850's, with narrow mourning border*

The nursery on the top floor of the Pavilion, directly above the Queen's sitting-room, was fully occupied from the time of the completion of the house until after the Prince's death. During this period children were a predominant feature of the Royal family's residence and these years were among the happiest of the Queen's long life. Yet this was something of a paradox, for though the Queen rejoiced in motherhood and adored the young children, she was not really a motherly person when it came to understanding the adolescent mind, which brought problems she could not easily contend with.

I see the children much less & even here . . . I find no special pleasure or compensation in the company of the elder children. You will remember that I told you this at Osborne. Usually they go out with me in the afternoon . . . and then only very occasionally do I find the rather intimate intercourse with them either agreeable or easy. You will not understand this, but it is caused by various factors. Firstly, I only feel properly *à mon aise* & quite happy when Albert is with me; secondly, I am used to carrying on all my many affairs quite alone; & then I have grown up all alone, accustomed to the society of adult (& never with younger) people – lastly, I still cannot get used to the fact that Vicky is almost grown up. To me, she still seems the same child, who had to be kept in order & therefore must not become too intimate . . .[1]

Lady Lyttelton, the first Superintendent of the Royal Children, was appointed in 1842. She was a widow of intelligence and humour and fully understood the nature of her duties with the Royal family – and of her charges:

The Princess Royal was most tender and touching in her regrets at leaving me; quite like few grown-up friends, and if at the last moment she had not quarrelled with her bonnet and tried to bite my hand in her rage I should take it all for steady affection.[2]

When the Princess Royal was seven her education was placed in the hands of a Miss Hildyard, a clergyman's daughter, and in the next few years the teaching staff increased rapidly to keep pace with the demands of the increasing number of children, and instructors were engaged for the special subjects: music, singing, drawing and sketching, and needlework, which were the accomplishments expected of any young lady. The Royal children all learned to ride at Osborne and Windsor.

The going was not always easy. The Prince of Wales was simply eclipsed by the brilliance of the Princess Royal's mind. Under the stress of a sense of inferiority and lack of confidence his behaviour deteriorated, and Osborne was the scene of many terrible tantrums when the Prince was smothered under the crushing educational system devised by Prince Albert's adviser, Baron Stockmar: 'If he does not like books, he must be made to like them.' The private diary of Mr. F. W. Gibbs, the Prince's tutor in 1852, describes some scenes in the schoolroom on the first floor of the Pavilion:

*Jan. 27* . . . In the morning it was difficult to fix his attention on his arithmetic. The music with Mrs. Anderson was not a good lesson. In the evening I read the story of Robert Bruce to him. I was astonished by the eager interest he took in it . . .

*Jan. 29* . . . Mr. Leitch the Drawing Master came. P. of W. very angry with P. Alfred and pulled his hair brandishing a paper-knife . . . Out walking I joined their play. The amusement is to act a play . . . fighting, brigands, knights, etc., form the chief personages – generally the chief part taken by himself.

*Feb. 28* . . . Last Thursday the two sons of Mr. Van de Weyer came to play with the Princes. They were eager and excited.

Afterwards I had to do some arithmetic with the P. of W. Immediately he became passionate, the pencil was flung to the end of the room, the stool was kicked away, and he was hardly able to apply at all. That night he woke twice. Next day he became very passionate because I told him he must not take out a walking-stick, and in consequence of something crossing him when dressing. Later in the day he became violently angry because I wanted some Latin done. He flung things about – made grimaces – called me names, and would not do anything for a long time.

*March 8.* A very bad day. The P. of W. has been like a person half silly. I could not gain his attention. He was very rude, particularly in the afternoon, throwing stones in my face. During his lesson in the morning, he was running first in one place, then in another. He made faces and spat. Dr. Becher complained of his great naughtiness. There was a great deal of bad words.[3]

The education of nine Royal children exercised many interested and intelligent minds. Lady Lyttelton was succeeded in 1851 by Lady Caroline Barrington, also a widow, and daughter of a former Prime Minister, Earl Grey. She continued in office until 1875, when Princess Beatrice was 18, and the Queen's grandchildren were appearing in increasing numbers at Osborne.

Queen Victoria insisted on a naturalness and simplicity in their upbringing and cherished the cultivation, so seldom achieved, of a complete trust between parents and children. She longed to be the perfect mother, but while she always tried sincerely to do her best by her children, her own temperament often defeated her efforts by too rigid an insistence on *principle* without regard to circumstances. As the Royal children grew older the Queen's lack of tact became more marked when she criticised them, but at least she could never be blamed for lack of interest in their welfare.

The children led sheltered, but in some ways, rather insecure, lives. They were often on the move from residence to Royal residence, and both their parents were intensely active, often away from home. Family separations were always upsetting on both sides:

*Friday, August 8, 1845* – A very fine morning when we got up. Both Vicky and darling Alice were with me when I dressed. Poor, dear Puss would much have wished to go with us . . . All four children were with us at breakfast – after which I gave Lady Lyttelton my last instructions, and then with a heavy heart we bade them all adieu in the Hall. Poor little Vicky seemed very sorry but did not cry . . . It was a very painful moment to drive away with the three poor little things standing at the door. Our dear Osborne is so lovely that we left it with the greatest regret.[4]

As the Royal children grew older they were brought downstairs to the dining-room in the evening to sit quietly with their

*At Osborne, February 1854: Queen Victoria with (left to right) the Prince of Wales, the Princess Royal, Princess Alice and Prince Alfred.* (Photo Fenton)

parents before returning to the Nursery for bed, but often days could pass without a member of the Household setting eyes on them. Visitors commented favourably on their looks and charm, but there were few chances of becoming better acquainted: occasionally, the very privileged might call in at the Nursery.

They learned to swim down in the Bay. They used either the small pier or, later, the swimming-bath, an ingenious affair made from pontoons, with a wooden grating floor open to the sea. The beach was private and secluded: a small semi-circular pavilion with a simple wooden bench seat supported on iron dolphins was built for the Queen, who would sit there and watch the children playing on the sand.

It was here that she herself first bathed from a horse-drawn bathing-machine (which is now on view near the Swiss Cottage). Assisted by a bathing woman in the discreet twilight of the machine and cumbrously attired, she descended the steps into the sea, the horse waiting patiently up to its fetlocks in water. The Queen was delighted by the experience until she put her head under water, 'when I thought I should be stifled.' Often she repeated the exercise, but keeping her head well above the waves.

In the summertime the Queen would walk or drive down to the children's gardens laid out at the end of the 'High Walk', where she could listen to the sound of the sea and help them with their little plots. In a shed beside the gardens the children's implements and wheelbarrows stand clean and polished as if awaiting their owners. This was her great happiness: here she could forget the despatch boxes and the secretaries and the business of State: here she was a mother with a brood of little ones to keep her busy. That quiet glade at the end of the 'High Walk' today possesses an aura of extraordinary peace.

It must have seemed logical that these gardens might frame a proper, but miniature, house. Following an example which Prince Albert had seen on the Continent a Swiss chalet arrived, imported in sections and speedily erected on the site. It was presented to the children on their mother's birthday, 24 May, 1854. To the English eye it may seem a little out of place but it served an admirable purpose. The interior was scaled down to child-size in every detail, with a fully equipped kitchen and range. There was a doll's house grocer's called 'Spratt's', where the children learned the prices of goods. Their parents aimed to teach them the elements of self-sufficiency, and in time they learned to cook, and to entertain their parents when they came to tea. Family parties could be held there with an informality which could never be found at the House; and so the Swiss Cottage, so often referred to in the Queen's Journal, provided for her yet another avenue of escape from a world which fascinated, yet at times was almost beyond, her.

The Osborne scene was unique in its variety. In contrast to the events related, and interspersed amongst them, Emperors, statesmen and diplomats visited the Queen at Osborne. After they had gone the Queen reverted to her role as mother, and looked forward eagerly to the charades and theatricals in which members of the Household and the Royal children, too, joined eagerly. Entertainment in those days had to be provided from within the home, and concerts, recitals and amateur dramatics generated as much interest and excitement in their preparation as in their performance. The children themselves staged such entertainments on the occasion of their parents' birthdays; in 1858 the Queen recorded in a letter to the Princess Royal, recently married to the Crown Prince of Prussia:

On the afternoon of my birthday (which was a wet one) I received your dear letter of the 22nd with such dear, warm hearty expressions of love and affection for which 10000 thanks. . . .

After lunch the children played
1. Arthur and Alice a little duet.
2. Louise a little piece alone, fairly, but not in time.
3. Alice and Lenchen a duet beautifully.
4. Alice and Affie on the violin a little composition of his own – very pretty and of which he is not a little proud.
5. Alice a long – beautiful and very difficult Sonata by Beethoven. Arthur recited a German poem, and Lenchen and Louise have something to say – which however has not yet been said.

The only one of all the children, who neither drew, wrote, played or did anything whatever to show his affection – beyond buying for me a table in Ireland – was Bertie. Oh! Bertie alas! alas! That is too sad a subject to enter on.[5]

A unique advantage of Osborne as a quiet residence for the Queen was the private landing stage in the Bay. Here the Queen could arrive and depart without the ceremony, the crowds and the bunting which is the panoply of Royalty. Her anxieties over

*The Prince of Wales and Prince Alfred, Osborne, August 1853.* (Photo by Dr. Becker)

her eldest son did not long cloud the aura of that idyllic holiday: a few days after the concert the Queen was writing buoyantly:

> I think I shall sail this afternoon, and tomorrow morning we mean to sail across to Alverbank for breakfast. [Prince Alfred was then being coached for his examination for entry into the Royal Navy at an establishment near Gosport.]

Yesterday there was a grand tea at the Swiss Cottage – and imagine good Affie by way of amusement exhibiting his air pump and steam engine . . . to Grandmamma, the others and the little Greys – and pumping over himself and Arthur! Can't you see him. He dined with us last night and sat next to me. He is a dear, good, clever promising child – whom God may bless![6]

This is surely a picture of Osborne at its best, and the informality of the scenes is delightful. The Queen would drive down to the beach, and there, amid the seclusion of the pine trees, embark on the Royal Yacht; the quiet unostentatious trip across Spithead in the early morning sunshine, with the water smooth and clear; a family breakfast with a promising young son, and then back again to the beloved home, where there was the affection and security of husband and family.

At the landing pier was a small stone Italianate house and the narrow lawn between it and the shore was the scene of many a homecoming. The Queen wrote, on her return from a State visit to Cherbourg: 'At twenty minutes to five we landed at our peaceful Osborne . . . Dear Affie was on the pier, and we found all the other children, including Baby, (Princess Beatrice), standing at the door . . . We went to see Affie's table (of birthday presents) – entirely nautical. Albert was suffering with headache, the result of his speech. I joined him on the lawn in an hour, and then went with the children – Alice and I driving – to the Swiss Cottage, which was all decked out with flags in honour of Alfred's birthday. The children had lunched there. Alice, Affie and Mr. Cowell were the additions to our dinner party. The two little boys (Arthur and Leopold) appeared. A band played and after dinner we danced, with the three boys and three girls and the company, a merry country dance on the terrace.'[7]

At the end of August Queen Victoria and Prince Albert were again landing at the Bay, this time from a visit to Germany to Vicky, whom they had not seen since her marriage earlier that year. They learned that Prince Alfred had passed his examination into the Navy: he met his parents as they landed – 'in his middie's jacket, cap, and dirk, half-blushing and looking very happy. He is a little pulled from these three days' hard examinations, which only terminated today . . . We felt very proud . . .'[8]

And all this was followed by another parting. Affie was shortly

to go to sea in H.M.S. *Euryalus,* and soon the remainder of the family would go north to Balmoral. But these domestic records remain of a long reign and a full family life, stretching away to a new century, portraying the perennial joys and sorrows of parenthood.

*Prince Alfred (Duke of Edinburgh) in Midshipman's uniform, August 1858.* (Photo by Lake Price)

# Court Life

Quite apart from the hundreds of servants and staff living in the Royal residences there was the Court, the immediate retinue of ladies and gentlemen who attended to the Queen's affairs wherever she might be living. Some of these were political posts and their occupants were only required on important or State occasions, but the Private Secretaries, Assistant Secretaries, Grooms, Equerries and Ladies-in-Waiting lived a nomadic existence and were by no means always as comfortable as might be supposed. They were, of course, always subject to the Queen's movements and through force of circumstances all became great travellers. Efficiency was one quality they had in common; another was absolute dedication to the interests of their Royal Mistress. As they followed the annual pattern of events – Osborne, Balmoral, Windsor and back to Osborne, with digressions to the Continent – these people had their quarters in the Royal Train and the Royal Yacht. That the Queen knew them and their families intimately and maintained the whole elaborate organisation down to the minutest detail was in itself no mean feat.

The Queen was a capricious taskmaster; she could be, and often was, immensely thoughtful over the well-being of those around her. Telegrams would be sent flying to summon some member of a courtier's family and a genuine warm-hearted sympathy would flow from her in times of mourning. After *her* experience in 1861 no one understood bereavement better than herself. Yet she could be unfair in her demands especially where her own comfort was concerned. Before Prince Albert's death she accepted the idea of a member of the Court marrying with equanimity; after it, she fought tooth and nail to cling to those around her. Just as the idea of her youngest daughter, Princess Beatrice marrying, was quite unthinkable – she *needed* her, and the topic of marriage was not to be discussed in her presence – so the question of one of the Queen's ladies marrying was distasteful to her. To the Queen, marriage suggested a division of loyalties and smacked of ingratitude.

The Secretaries were in permanent attendance on the Queen and were usually lucky enough to be given a house near the Royal residences, so that their wives could be with them. Sir Henry Ponsonby, Private Secretary from 1870 until his death in 1895, was allotted the Norman Tower at Windsor Castle and Kent Cottage, and later, Osborne Cottage which still stands in York Avenue on the edge of the estate, in the Isle of Wight. Ponsonby loathed Balmoral – as did most of the Court – where there was no married accommodation available for him sufficiently near at hand to please the Queen, and he chafed under the separation, often as long as four months in the year, from his wife.

Equerries and Ladies-in-Waiting normally spent a month in waiting followed by three months of private life. The work was exacting, if not always onerous. Their chief complaint was that they never knew when they might be wanted and that much time was spent in enforced idleness. For Marie Mallet a morning's work consisted of writing two letters and drafting two telegrams. She lamented the hours spent alone in her room waiting for a summons that might not come and of the dreadful air of secrecy that surrounded the work of the Court. The Queen was the hub of it all, and the point was that they had always to be immediately available to her and she was loudly indignant if any one of them could not be found.

*Osborne. July 12 '85.*

The Queen *must* ask that both Sir Henry & Major Edwards sh$^d$ *not* be out on Sunday Mrg or any other *at the same time.* Not 5 minutes after the service in the Chapel was over she sent to say she wished to see Sir Henry in a $\frac{1}{4}$ of an hour but was told he was gone to church. She then sent for Major Edwards & was then told he was out too.

This is extremely inconvenient. . . . She must ask Sir Henry to take care that this does not happen again. . . .

There is now especially so much of a public & private nature wanting arrangement & *constant* attention (she) must have all the necessary assistance she requires, being quite done up with *all* her work and anxieties for the last 6 or 7 weeks. . . .[1]

The latter part of the Queen's note provides one key to the problem. She felt herself a weak and vulnerable old woman on her lonely eminence and quite unequal to the burden of sovereignty without the constant attendance of her trusted courtiers. Her apparent selfishness becomes more easily understandable if we remind ourselves that, deprived of the extraordinary ability and moral support of Prince Albert at the early age of forty-two, she had struggled on alone bereft of the one man upon whom she could utterly rely. There could be no substitute for the Prince and she was continually guided in her decision-making by his example – 'what Albert would have wished'.

The tedium of life at Court after the Prince's death was sometimes almost unimaginable. Days would pass without any of the Household save the dressers and the ladies-in-waiting seeing the Queen. When she went out for her drive they too were free to leave the house – but they must not be seen by the Queen and would take elaborate precautions against such a disaster. Balmoral provided the Queen with the means of a retreat from the affairs of State; the Castle itself proving too big, she would disappear attended only by a few servants to a remote cottage from which she would emerge refreshed. But at Windsor and Osborne the Court was nearer the centre of affairs and social life and visits were altogether easier. Ministers, who were spared the ordeal of a six-hundred mile journey to conduct their business, rejoiced and the Household breathed a sigh of relief. At Osborne the Royal yachts were kept busy plying between the mainland and Cowes or Osborne Bay with despatches and passengers; the evenings were made tolerable by concerts and recitals arranged for the Queen's entertainment. Most of the great artistes of the period are to be seen on the programmes: Signor Tosti, the de Reszkes, Clara Butt, Melba. Opera companies arrived to give a private performance. The Court got up their own theatricals and there were tableaux in which the Princes and Princesses took part.

Sometimes the Queen would attend the rehearsals, for she took the keenest interest in their progress, her eagle eye missing no detail. In later years she would be wheeled in by her Indian attendant and would start the performance by ringing a small

*Prince Arthur (Duke of Connaught) with Major Elphinstone, c. 1860*

gold hand-bell. Usually, though, the recitals were more informal; the Queen would send a message to one of the Household, requiring songs or music after dinner. In those days before
wireless and television the art of entertaining at home was far
more highly developed than it is today; the singing of a part at
sight and accompanying at the piano were normal accomplishments and it was expected that anyone would take his turn
without embarrassment.

But often the evenings at Osborne were very dull. A depressing silence hung like a pall over the house and even if any
member of the Household were dining with the Queen the meal
would be taken in a gloomy, forbidding atmosphere. There was
little conversation unless it was initiated by the Queen who
could, when she wished, prove an accomplished and witty racon-
teur. She would draw upon her vast fund of experience and recall
events involving people long since dead. Always she held the
reins tightly and she would administer a sharp snub to anyone
who presumed on her favour.

The hierarchy was a curious one. Immediately next to Queen
Victoria herself came Princess Alice, and later, Princess Beatrice. In turn they were the constant companions of the Queen,
the latter remaining in that capacity until her mother's death.
She transmitted the Queen's responses and reactions, read aloud
memoranda and State documents and, over the long years,
proved the indispensable link between her mother and nearly
everyone else. There was still, however, the mother and daughter
relationship which was bound to tinge every aspect of their life
together.

The Women of the Bedchamber in a quite different way ran
the Princess a close second. The most memorable of them, Lady
Jane Churchill and the Hon. Harriet Phipps, occupied a unique
position. These good ladies formed the link between the Queen
and her daughter and the Court, and the need for tactful hand-
ling of elderly gentlemen was very great. Upon them devolved
much of the work inherent in the Queen's private life; Miss
Phipps was also known as Queen Victoria's personal secretary,
and their role was an intrinsic part of what was essentially a
female establishment.

The actual work varied enormously in both content and quan-
tity. All State matters were dealt with by the Private Secretaries.
They had to be strictly non-party men, for they saw a long suc-

cession of Tory and Liberal governments come and go. Ponsonby developed his office to a fine art. He was attentive, alert and watchful, content to remain in the background and, from his conversations with visiting statesmen, gained vast experience, second only probably to the Queen's, of the political machine. He preferred his Sovereign's approval to the conferment of honours and with his shrewd knowledge of his Royal Mistress, his wit and wisdom, he was able to enliven the dullness of Court life. As Secretary he was deeply concerned with the Queen's relationships with her great family on the Continent. On most matters the Queen had decided views of her own but Ponsonby's quiet advice to Ministers was often sought.

While much of the actual work was concerned with correspondence, and the drafting and deciphering of telegrams, there was a vital social role to be fulfilled as well. Visitors to the Court and members of the Royal family were to be met, accommodated, entertained and despatched with faultless efficiency. The whole Household shared in this duty which was rendered more than usually complicated by the Queen's habit of writing endless notes. Inevitably, despite her concern for trivial detail, much depended on the initiative of her Household. On one occasion Ponsonby's son, 'Fritz', was concerned by the appearance of a strange and rather wild-looking German demanding to see the Empress Frederick, the Queen's eldest daughter, on her arrival at Cowes. He decided that the man was a lunatic and took steps to protect the Empress. Ponsonby was much put out when he learned that the man was well known to the Empress in Berlin as a sculptor, and that he was in fact expected by her. Nevertheless, with his scanty knowledge of the facts he was right to take precautions. In earlier years there had been four attempts on Queen Victoria's life, and others on Royalty on the Continent.

Members of the Household tended to be drawn from a select, rather narrow circle and heredity played no small part in the Queen's choice. It was natural enough; if a father suited the Queen, she would tend to invite the son to accept an appointment as Equerry in the fullness of time; a daughter might join the Household as a Maid of Honour. A natural tendency for these young people to marry proved a recurring inconvenience to the Queen which was more deeply resented as she became older. In 1894 the Queen appointed Frederick Ponsonby Equerry to give a pleasant surprise to his father, Sir Henry, then in his last year as her Private Secretary. Sir Frederick, as he became, was promoted in 1897 to Assistant Private Secretary and served the two succeeding Sovereigns.

In 1887 Queen Victoria appointed Marie Adeane Maid of Honour. She was the daughter of one of her former Ladies-in-Waiting, Lady Elizabeth Biddulph, and niece of the Hon. Alec Yorke, then an Assistant Secretary. Marie resigned four years later in order to marry Bernard Mallet; the Queen forgave what she considered monstrous ingratitude and sent her a handsome wedding-present. Four years later Marie was offered, and accepted, the post of Extra Woman of the Bedchamber, under the Hon. Harriet Phipps, and remained in Royal service until the Queen's death.

In *Life with Queen Victoria* Victor Mallet has compiled some of his mother's letters from Court; they reveal a portrait of a lively and intelligent young woman and also provide an insight into the somewhat sombre aura of majesty surrounding the Queen.

*From Osborne, 22 December, 1887.*

A huge royal footman met me at the Cowes pier and looked straight over my humble head till I suggested that I was Miss Adeane, whereupon he seized my bag and whisked me off to a royal brougham which speedily deposited me here, the House-keeper in black kid gloves greeted me most kindly and showed me my room, and very soon Miss Phipps carried me off to tea and she and Lady Churchill were most kind . . . I dine with the Queen tonight . . .[2]

On the 27th she wrote: 'After dining with the Household we were toasting our toes when suddenly Prince Henry appeared and after announcing that the ladies were to go to the Drawing Room the Prince came up to me and said: "You are to sing." I turned pea-green and stammered: "I really can't, sir," and with much confusion explained that I was prepared to play but that my voice was feeble and that I never sang in public: it was alarming but I think I was right for without anyone to accompany me and shaking with fright I should have broken down to a certainty; so he told the Queen and I was let off; however, I had to read a horrid duet with Princess Beatrice, the Queen sitting close by; I believe I got through it pretty well but I could hardly see the notes and simply prayed for the end.'[3]

Being in the Queen's presence could be a terrifying or an amusing experience, for she was unpredictable and captious in her requirements. It was to Uncle Alec Yorke, after he had repeated at her request a slightly risqué story, that she addressed her famous quelling remark, 'We are not amused.' At other times she would laugh suddenly and uproariously at a slight comment. Sir Henry Ponsonby was heard to remark that people laughed at his conversation when he had not intended to be funny. After dinner it was customary for the ladies, headed by the Queen, to withdraw, and the gentlemen remained behind to drink port. Prince Albert did not usually stay long; he had no common background with many of his Household, having been brought up in Coburg, and joined the more congenial company of the ladies after a short interval. The menfolk tended to linger in the more relaxed atmosphere: they came from much the same social circle, shared the same friends and had many experiences in common. Being ingenious and intelligent they helped to make the long evenings more tolerable. Marie Mallet told her mother:

> . . . I dined with the Household but at ten we all marched into the Drawing Room and were stared at until $\frac{1}{4}$ to 11, when the Queen having been safely seen upstairs, we adjourned to the Council Room and danced on a carpet, to the sound of a piano mechanique turned alternately by the Duchess of Albany, (the widow of Prince Leopold), and Col. Carrington. It was really very comical, Prince Henry (of Battenberg) got tremendously excited and pranced about all over the place, he nearly whirled me off my legs, for he dances in the German fashion and plunges horribly . . . At last (after playing Consequences) about 1 o'clock breathless with laughter we retired to rest, having quite enjoyed ourselves, a somewhat rare event in these regions . . .'[4]

The tableaux and amateur theatricals were greatly looked forward to. Rehearsals and the preparation of costumes occupied many leisure hours, and the Queen, who enjoyed them immensely, gave them her blessing, often attending rehearsals. On January 6, 1888, three tableaux were presented with Prince and Princess Henry of Battenberg in the leading roles, supported by members of the Household. They were 'The Queen of Sheba',

'Carmen' and 'Queen Elizabeth and Raleigh', and apparently a great success.

What Marie Mallet described as a 'deadly level of caution and dullness' was the result of the need to exercise extraordinary discretion and tact. Towards the end of the Queen's reign the Secretaries were upset by the knowledge that despatches were being read to her by some of her Ladies. It was not surprising in view of the Queen's failing eyesight, but it caused a disturbance in the even tenor of Court life.

The periods of waiting were arranged by Miss Phipps and the Queen. Windsor was popular among the Household, but Balmoral was cordially detested on account of its remoteness and tedium, especially when the Queen had retired to one or another of the remote 'shiels' and there was little to do at the Castle. Osborne in winter could be bitterly cold. There was a heavy snow-storm in February, 1900, and the Queen did not go out for her usual drive – an almost unheard of departure from custom. From about this time the duties of the Ladies became more onerous: the Queen's increasing difficulty in sleeping at night played havoc with her routine. She would doze off in her carriage and in the Drawing-Room, and it became more difficult than ever to keep her awake. Her companions rustled newspapers and dropped their fans; they talked in urgent tones, but often to no avail. Then the Queen would lie awake half the night with similar effects on the following day.

Those who were privileged to be in close attendance on the Queen during the last years of her reign were profoundly impressed by her grasp of affairs, her thoughtfulness to those about her, and her stoicism in the face of personal bereavement; perhaps more than any of these, her unfailing interest in the course of the Boer War and in the wounded who lay at Netley, on the other side of the Solent, was proof of her indomitable will to carry out her duties as Sovereign. No one, observing this tenacity of purpose, could fail to be proud of being in the Queen's personal service.

## Barton Manor

After Queen Victoria's acquisition of Osborne she set about enlarging the estate to double its original size by purchase of suitable land. To the north-west lay Norris Castle, that former haunt of the Queen's childhood, with its own frontage to the Solent, its grass sweeping down to the water. On the south-east, the neighbouring estate was Barton Manor, a fair-sized farm with a residence in need of some repair. It, too, had its own waterfront adjacent to that of Osborne and when it came into the market the Queen promptly snapped it up, delighted and somewhat awed by the size of her possessions, which now gave her some real privacy.

Barton lay a mile distant from Osborne barely visible across the parkland. As one of the Queen's properties it never really came into its own as Frogmore did at Windsor, or York Cottage at Sandringham. King George V, when Prince of Wales, occupied it briefly in 1908 and 1909 on visits to his sons at the Naval College. In Queen Victoria's day Barton was used to accommodate the overspill from Osborne. It was for years the residence of the Equerries but the house never found much favour in their eyes. It was a gloomy building with tall Tudor-style chimneys, and had the reputation of being haunted. Furthermore, it suffered from the distinct disadvantage of being too far from Osborne for walking on a wet evening when the Household assembled in knee-breeches and silk stockings. A brougham called at Barton before dinner to bring the gentlemen across.

The scene comes vividly to the mind: the cold rain slanting down on to the dark, silent house whose corridors were dimly lit by oil lamps in bowls; the horse-drawn carriage trotting up the drive and the narrow wheels crunching on the gravel to come to a halt at the Household Entrance to the right of the quadrangle fronting the Pavilion wing. The gentlemen emerge swathed in their cloaks, nod to the draped coachman on the box and hurry indoors. The Equerries who have been notified beforehand that they are to dine with the Queen assemble and walk slowly down the chilly corridor with its floor of mosaic and its marble statues and busts, icy-cold, lining the walls. They converse in hushed tones; an almost uncanny silence pervades the house. At the end of the corridor they turn to the left and enter the short passage leading to the Entrance Hall, more brightly lit but only a degree warmer than the long corridor, for the Queen intensely disliked warm rooms. A door opens silently, there is a murmur of voices; the Equerries pass through blinking at the sudden blaze of light from the candelabra and mirrors in the Drawing-Room and the door closes. The lamps burn steadily though the flames waver in the slight draughts.

At the other end of the house, the remainder of the Household sit down to dinner in their own Dining-Room. The conversation is general and relaxed, witty and intelligent, ranging from the arts to current affairs, for part of the duty of every member of the Household is to keep himself well informed. Forthcoming theatricals or tableaux are discussed light-heartedly. After dinner some of the gentlemen adjourn to the billiard-room to smoke, others make their way down the corridor connecting the two wings to the Council Room for a rehearsal. When the Queen has retired the Equerries living at Barton send for their carriage; donning their cloaks they stand by the door. Sir Frederick Ponsonby recalls that one evening whilst waiting for the brougham he was showing a friend how the statues could revolve on their plinth. Using 'Psyche' for illustration he turned her but the statue overbalanced and they were unable to prevent the heavy block of marble from crashing to the mosaic floor. Footmen were summoned but their united efforts could not raise it. When Ponsonby reported the matter to the Queen she was greatly displeased and circulated to her Household a note to the effect that 'they were not to touch the statues and certainly not play with them,' which surprised a number of staid, elderly ladies who had not learnt of the episode.

The brougham drives up, the Equerries climb in and the vehicle moves off out of the small circle of light. As it circles the corner of the house the sound of the horses' hooves and the rumble of the wheels is abruptly cut off. Upstairs in the Pavilion the Queen, assisted by her dresser, is in bed. The lamps burn on in the corridors and in the offices of the night staff. Across the fields at Barton, the Equerries bid one another good-night and, collecting their candles, light themselves upstairs.

# 6

## 'Day turned into Night'

The year 1861 proved a turning-point in the Queen's life. It began with the death of one of her numerous distant relatives but plans were afoot for family weddings: the Prince of Wales's engagement to Princess Alexandra and Princess Alice's marriage to Prince Louis of Hesse-Darmstadt were looked forward to for the following year. On the 16 March, however, the Queen was shattered by the death of her mother, the Duchess of Kent, at Frogmore, after an operation, though she had been suffering from cancer for as long as six years. The Queen was prostrated and this in itself may be a cause of wonder to those who recall the strained relationships between mother and daughter at the time of the Queen's accession. In fact, a reconciliation had been effected since the Queen's marriage; her children had been the subject of tender thoughts and letters and a sort of confidence had long been established. The Queen's almost excessive grief therefore stemmed more from the events of the distant past – she felt that remorse which comes from an inability to put back the clock. In a sense, the recent happiness in their communication only made matters worse. Prince Albert carried her in his arms from the death-bed and she retired from public life, her seclusion remaining almost unbroken until the next disaster, the death of the Prince Consort in December. She wrote:

> I cried constantly yesterday . . . and when we all entered the breakfast room (on Princess Alice's birthday) I felt as if my heart must break! Not one day these weary 6 weeks have I passed without tears – and very often cry bitterly still! It seems very long since I saw her – and heard from her – and so it must go on for the rest of my life! It seems a fearful thought . . .
> It was a very fine day – very hot sun – everything so green – the trees nearly out – profusion of primroses and violets, king-

cups – anemones – oxlips etc. – and the nightingales singing beautifully. In the afternoon we drove in the small char à banc but the noise of the wheels on the roads hurts me very much; Alice has driven me every morning in the little Sardinian pony carriage which with india rubber wheels makes no noise.[1]

★

The death of the Prince Consort on 14 December drastically changed the course of the Queen's life. A woman of passionate and ardent temperament, she had failed to recognise the signs of deterioration in her husband's health and lacked the self-control over her impatience, obstinacy and wilfulness which might have saved him. During the three years before his death his spirit was on the wane and little was required to extinguish completely his frail spark of life.

In the first months of 1858 he lost the affectionate and intellectual companionship of his eldest daughter, Vicky, when she left England to live in Prussia with her husband, 'Fritz'. She was the one person in whom the Prince could confide on a level that matched his own; the one, moreover, who could draw him out and do more to help him overcome the morbid introspective part of himself than anyone alive. Referring to the 'void' left after her departure he wrote: '. . . yet not in my heart, for there assuredly you will abide henceforth . . . , but in my daily life, which is evermore reminding my heart of your absence.'[2]

The Queen's emotions were stirred no less deeply, perhaps, than the Prince's: '. . . A dreadful day. Such sickness came over me, real heartache, when I thought of our dearest child being gone, and for so long – all, all being over! . . . At times I could be quite cheerful, but my tears began to flow afresh frequently, and I could not go near Vicky's corridor . . .'[3]

The fact remained, however, that the Queen could still depend utterly upon her husband and, much as she regretted the parting and remained a close correspondent with her daughter, she was not so bereft as the Prince by her departure. A tragic irony was a feature of the match. It had been a political marriage arranged by the Queen and the Prince when Vicky was only fourteen. They had always realised that it would be necessary for her to live abroad; they could hardly have known that it was to prove an intrinsic factor in the Prince's decline.

During the course of that year the Prince led a full and active life, and was able to visit his daughter, but his physical health was a cause of almost constant anxiety. In the following year Prince Albert became a grandfather at the age of forty, which gave him much happiness, but he continued to be grossly overworked and the Queen's importunate demands on him, as well as those from Ministers and public institutions, gave him little or no respite.

The death of the Duchess of Kent early in 1861 threw an added strain upon the Prince. Not only he, but the Royal Physician, feared for the balance of the Queen's mind. Her paroxysms of grief seemed excessive even for an age which was notoriously demonstrative. The Prince Consort was worried and exasperated. Upon him fell the burden of carrying out public duties which in themselves imposed a burden on him and took their toll of his health. His digestion was considerably impaired and was not improved by his returning home to a distraught wife. He had not even Vicky to console him.

Two other blows struck him in that same fateful year. An epidemic of typhoid broke out in the Portuguese Royal family and, within a few days of one another, King Pedro and his brother, Prince Ferdinand, cousins of Prince Albert's, had died of the fever. The Prince was shocked by the double blow for he had developed a great respect for this enlightened king of a backward and deprived country during his recent visit to England. He suffered increasingly from insomnia; an entry in his diary reveals that he scarcely slept for a fortnight after the tragedy.

Almost simultaneously another disaster occurred. News reached him that the Prince of Wales had been involved in an escapade while serving with the Guards at the Curragh Camp, Dublin. An actress named Nellie Clifden had been smuggled into his quarters at night. As the news leaked out the Prince Consort felt that he had been betrayed by his son. He experienced an acute sense of failure; his aspirations for the integrity of his son, for so many years in doubt, had fallen headlong and, again, he had no one to whom he could turn. He wrote to Baron Stockmar, his old adviser: 'I am fearfully in want of a true friend and counsellor, and that *you* are the friend and counsellor I want, you will readily understand.'[4] But Stockmar was old and infirm and had some years ago retired to his native Germany, never to return.

At any other time, or if his health had not already been shaken, he would not have allowed it [the Curragh episode] to weight unduly upon his spirits. As it was, however, he was unable to shake it off. It haunted him with the persistency with which even trifles haunt the mind, when the nervous system has been overtaxed.[5]

On the same day the Queen noted that the Prince was 'low and sad',[6] and although he conscientiously attended to his duties it was clear to those who knew him that these crushing blows had gone deep. By now, not only was his physical resistance to infection weakened, but also he lacked the will-power to fight. Not long before his death he told the Queen, 'I do not cling to life. You do; but I set no store by it. If I knew that those I love were well cared for, I should be quite ready to die tomorrow.' He added, 'I am sure, if I had a severe illness, I should give up at once, I should not struggle for life. I have no tenacity of life.'[7] It is doubtful whether this is merely an expression of the Prince's religious beliefs in a life hereafter; it has the tone of a man who lacks the innate instinct for survival, or in whom that instinct has been lost. Even the Queen remarked on it; he seemed not to care to live . . . 'He died from want of what they call pluck'.[8]

The cause of the Prince's last illness cannot be finally ascertained. Typhoid was more or less endemic a hundred years ago and especially in areas where the drainage system was in poor condition. At Windsor this was lamentably true, despite the Prince's efforts to carry out a programme of improvement and modernisation. At all events, the first symptoms appeared a few days after visiting the construction work at the Royal Military College, Sandhurst, on a day of incessant rain. A week later, on 1 December, the Prince was still attempting to lead a normal life but was far from well. He neither ate nor slept, and he complained of feeling as if cold water was being poured down his back. He became increasingly restless and moved from his bed to a sofa. On the 8th his condition seemed to have improved but by the 12th the fever returned.

It seems probable that by this time the Prince had exhausted what little fight had been left in him. He told Princess Alice that he was dying. On the 13th and 14th his life flickered, at times seeming almost to glow more brightly and keeping hope alive.

During the course of the 14th, however, he was clearly sinking and, at a quarter to eleven, surrounded by the Queen and his family, he died.

## 7

## A Widow's Seclusion

Five days after the death of the Prince Consort the distraught Queen retreated to the Isle of Wight. Already severely depressed by her mother's death a few months earlier, Queen Victoria became almost frantic with grief. Eighteen months before the Prince's death the Queen had expressed the hope that she would not survive him; now this had come, terrifying and calamitous. At times she burst into hysterical weeping but though she gradually became calmer, she was for more than ten years unable to record the full account of the Prince's death in her Journal. At the time the most she could manage were a few jotted notes. To King Leopold she wrote: 'My *life* as a *happy* one is *ended*! The world is gone for *me*! . . . CUT OFF at forty-two . . . is *too awful*, too cruel!'[1]

At Osborne, the Queen withdrew almost completely. At first, she would see no one; she ate alone; Princess Alice was her sole companion, and it was she who saw to it that a line of communication with the Government was maintained. For a time the Queen feared that she would lose her reason. Very gradually, however, almost imperceptibly, she began to take a more outward view. Less than a month after the Prince's death the Queen sent a message of sympathy and a gift of £200 to the widows of the victims of a colliery disaster in Northumberland. Soon afterwards she agreed to receive the Prime Minister.

The truth is that the Queen without the Prince was utterly lost. She had been more dependent on him than could seem possible; he had been referred to on every point of her life and had been her sole arbiter of judgment and taste. She resumed the business of State soon after arriving at Osborne, and she grappled bravely with documents which seemed to defy comprehension but which Albert would have unravelled for her. At every turn she felt her inadequacy. For the rest of her life the

Prince remained for her the symbol of perfection. There came over her an iron determination always to be governed in accordance with his own principles. 'Albert would have wished it' became her theme. Again she wrote to her uncle: '. . . *his* wishes – *his* plans – about everything, *his* views about *every* thing are to be my *law*! And no human power will make me swerve from *what he* decided and wished . . . *No one* person,' she continued, '. . . is to lead or guide or dictate *to me*.'[2] (from Osborne, 24 December, 1861).

This letter, written while the first acute pangs of grief still assailed her, affords a clue perhaps to the Queen's reputation for obstinacy. Nothing could shake her opinion on a subject once it had been formed: she saw defeat as a humiliation. Often immense tact was required in the shaping of her views: a hasty remark could shatter the result of long and tactful negotiation.

So she received the Prime Minister, her former enemy, Lord Palmerston. Attired in voluminous black crape, she was not pleased to note his new-found briskness – he had lately recovered from gout – and cheerful attire of brown overcoat, light grey trousers, green gloves and blue studs. Even so, a certain attachment had developed from the wranglings of the past, and she dreaded at this time a change of government – and a change was due at any moment.

But there were many other matters to occupy her during these long and weary hours. She conceived it her duty to establish memorials wherever possible to her idol, whose wise counsel she had during her whole reign unquestioningly followed. There were statues and busts to be commissioned; cairns and obelisks to be ordered; she gave instructions that Albert's clothes were still to be put out as if for him, and hot water was to be brought to his room. The Mausoleum at Frogmore was sited – the Queen and Princess Alice chose the spot on 18 December – and planned; it was to be light, airy and beautiful and, like Osborne, with something of the Italianate about it.

For two months the Queen did not stir from Osborne, such was her utter prostration. Though afterwards she moved about the country, following the familiar routine, she scarcely appeared in public and took no part in State ceremonial. It was not until 1864 that she attended a public function or drove in an open carriage. The public, who expected to *see* the Queen, might be forgiven the creeping rumour that she was about to abdicate:

But this was to misunderstand the Queen. Such an action would have been incompatible with Prince Albert's notions of duty; moreover, it was incompatible with her own assessment of her situation. In 1863 she wrote to Theodore Martin, author of *The Life of the Prince Consort*: 'It is not the Queen's *sorrow* that keeps her secluded . . . it is her *overwhelming work* and her health . . . From the hour she gets out of bed till she gets into it again there is work, work, work, – letter-boxes, questions, etc., which are dreadfully exhausting – and if she had not comparative rest and quiet in the evening she would most likely not be *alive*. Her brain is constantly overtaxed.'[3]

The exact truth is difficult to discern. We cannot really believe that, struck down as she was, the Queen could have carried on a full public life such as she had sustained in previous years. Undeniably, she was almost submerged not only by the mass but, also, the complexity, of the State papers which continued to arrive, and which the Prince had guided her through with so unerring a hand. Probably, a combination of these factors – health affected by grief, work affected by health, and the sheer magnitude of the task – formed a vicious circle which was by and large to keep her out of the public eye for so many years.

Meanwhile, the silence of the tomb seemed to descend upon the house at Osborne. Voices were muted, laughter was hushed, footfalls were muffled. The Queen, a small, impenetrably lonely figure, laboured on. At Osborne and, later, at Balmoral especially, everything around Queen Victoria served to remind her of the Prince's handiwork. It was *he* who had ordered and arranged and laid out, who had lived to see his plans come to fruition but not to enjoy for long the results. It now became the Queen's steadfast intention that the public should be taught to appreciate the Prince: if he was the model of perfection as she was in her own mind convinced, then her subjects should have that model ever before them to guide them in their own aspirations.

With this in mind Queen Victoria commissioned two biographies of the Prince: General Grey's, published in 1866, and Martin's which appeared in five volumes between 1874 and 1880. Martin's was the more comprehensive, but both were sympathetic, presenting a portrait of the ideal as it had appeared to the Queen. Unhappily, the great majority of the public did not want the ideal and did not like what it saw; and it has taken several generations to create a more realistic character-study of the

man who was Queen Victoria's husband. If Martin depicts the
Prince's grasp of intellectual affairs, his sense of duty, imagin-
ation, industry and affection, more recent study reveals the man
behind the image: a man who had lost his mother early in life and
who had been marked by this unhappy experience – for he was
not always clever in his dealings with women; a man prone to
morbid introspection and anxious about his health; a father who,
in his insistence on study and the cultivation of the mind, failed
to recognise in his son, Bertie, the need for affection, and warped
his childhood. In the end his death from typhoid fever resulted as
much from his own passive acceptance of his condition as from
physical, mental and spiritual exhaustion.

★

The following summer, safely delivered of her third child,
Vicky came to England, and was at last reunited with her
grief-stricken mother. Eleanor Stanley describes her arrival:

> At 11 punctually the *Victoria and Albert* lay off Osborne Pier
> and the Crown Princess of Prussia and her suite landed in
> boats. Lady Jocelyn, who went with Princess Alice to the pier
> to meet her, but remained at the end, to let the two sisters have
> a few moments to themselves, says that both cried, but not
> very much, Princess Alice most, at first meeting; but that the
> Princess Royal soon composed herself, and walked up the pier,
> with the tears still on her cheeks, but with striking dignity and
> composure, shook hands with them all, and got into the car-
> riage to drive up to Osborne, quite calmly . . .[4]

For the Princess, who had not witnessed her father's last illness, there must have been a shocking unreality in the situation
as she found it at Osborne. There were her father's hat and coat,
hung up as though he had just come in from a walk; his walking-
stick was where he had left it in the umbrella-stand; his clothes
were laid out ready for him in his dressing-room – all gave her
the impression that he was still with them. Eleanor Stanley,
coming to the end of her waiting, noted:

> The Queen admitted me after dinner to take leave: she looked
> sadly worn and thinned and very small altogether with her

widow's cap . . . and her heavy clinging woollen gown . . . She
was standing in the middle of his dressing room, where his
wash-hand stand and things were all arranged, as though
ready for him, (not, however, set out on the dressing table, as I
had heard). She sleeps tolerably well in general.[5]

All seemed as it had been − all save the presence of that warm
personality whom she had so deeply loved − for Vicky had perhaps been closer to her father than any other of his children. It
was hard to accept that life went on just the same, harder still
that Osborne − her whole life, indeed − would never be the same
again. A year ago she had written: 'how I miss him whom I wor-
shipped, his step, his dear dear voice, his beloved face . . .'[6] and it
was at this homecoming that she felt all the agony of separation
most acutely.

Queen Victoria's reaction to the Prince Consort's death was,
even in her life time, and has been since, the subject of much comment. We tend to forget the keenness of Victorian senti-
mentality: public manifestations of grief on the occasion of a
death in the family were widely observed and respected. Blinds
were drawn, black crape was tied to the knocker, and the wearing of mourning for prescribed periods evoked expressions of
sympathy which the books on etiquette laid down. If we wonder
why the Queen went to such pains to provide herself with daily
reminders of the Prince's absence: his watch-pocket hanging on
his side of the bed, his possessions all in their places and meticulously maintained; why Osborne remained her favourite home,
which he had done so much to create, we may find the answer in
the Queen's surrender to him, a surrender total and absolute, so
that she could not so much as choose a hat without him. The
Prince's death had deprived her at a stroke of his support and
counsel, and she was numbed by the prospect of carrying alone
the immense burdens of sovereignty and family life.

## 8

## Princess Alexandra at Osborne – 1862

Two months after the Prince of Wales had become betrothed to Princess Alexandra she arrived at Osborne to spend a few weeks with her future mother-in-law. At this time the Queen was still in deep mourning for the Prince Consort, the house was silent and cheerless, like a tomb, with icy white marble statues of Albert in the corridors, and everything just as it had been before his death. It was a house without laughter and, less than a year since 'the light went out of her life', shrouded in grief.

The scene had been carefully set for the visit. The Prince of Wales had been sent off on a cruise of the Mediterranean, for the Queen wished to have Alexandra to herself. The Princess's father, Prince Christian of Denmark, himself was to stay only two days: for the rest the Queen was to be free to mould her as the Princess of Wales. Whatever Bertie and Prince Christian may have thought the Queen's wish was law.

The visit began well with the Princess and her father met at Trinity Pier by Lenchen and the nine year old Prince Leopold. It was already dark as the carriage drove up the avenue to the house where the Queen, accompanied by Louise and Beatrice, awaited them. Later, the three grown-ups and Lenchen dined together in the Council Room.[1] The evening went well; the Queen was gracious, Alexandra had come prepared to please, and it was not long before she had thoroughly endeared herself to the stricken widow.

The following day was wet but twenty-four hours later, when Prince Christian was to take his departure, it cleared up sufficiently for the Queen to drive out with the Princess in the grounds. By the evening it was blowing a gale, and raining heavily, and Alexandra was left alone. It was an arduous task that lay before her, just how arduous she was to discover as the years went by, but on this visit she listened attentively to the Queen who expounded the way of life of the consort of the heir to the Throne. By the end of the visit the Queen, warmed by the Princess's demonstrative sympathy for her in her affliction, was to call her 'this jewel'. Even after she had been at Osborne only a week the Queen wrote of her to Vicky: 'I can't say how I and we all love her! She is so good, so simple, unaffected, frank, bright and cheerful, yet so quiet and gentle that her *umgang* (companionship) soothes me. Then *how* lovely . . . this jewel! She is *one* of those sweet creatures who seem to come from the skies to help and bless poor mortals and lighten for a time their path!' In her Journal, written on the same day, the Queen added: 'How beloved Albert would have loved her!'[2]

The Princess was no fool, however. She used to recall with amusement those three weeks spent with the Queen both at Osborne and, later, at Windsor, when she had been a pupil and very much on approval, and had come to understand and love Queen Victoria. But she would recall, too, that her mother, from whom she had never previously been parted, had not been invited to England, and that her father, when he returned to fetch her home, could not be found room at Windsor Castle but was obliged to put up at the Danish Embassy. The reason for this may be found in the insistence of the Princess's mother in having her daughter home in time for her birthday, and the Queen, though supported in her efforts to keep Alix by the Prince of Wales, was compelled to give way. There is perhaps something selfish and inconsiderate in the Queen's outlook: they were traits which tended to harden as she entered into old age. Yet it was understandable: the Queen knew her son; she remembered all too clearly the Curragh Camp incident, and feared the effects of the fecklessness and unbookish tendencies of the Prince, while not allowing sufficiently for his very real charm. She did not want to lose her 'jewel', and longed to keep her; to enjoy her warmth of heart and to train her in her future role.

# John Brown

No account of Queen Victoria's life at Osborne would be complete without mention of John Brown, her Scottish personal attendant. Brown, a strong, handsome man in his thirties, was chosen by the Prince Consort to be the Queen's particular gillie. He quickly proved handy, adaptable and resourceful and his coolness in emergency on the occasion of an accident to the Queen's carriage brought him into prominence. In 1864, while the Queen was still nervy and weak from the tragedy of Prince Albert's death, Brown came down to Osborne for the winter to act as her groom.

Promotion came quickly to Brown: In 1865 he was appointed 'The Queen's Highland Servant'; by 1872 he had become 'Esquire' and his salary had more than trebled. Even in the early days Queen Victoria found herself able to write enthusiastically to Vicky: 'He is so quiet, has such an excellent head and memory. . . . I feel I have here always in the House a good, devoted Soul . . . whose only object and interest is my service.'[1] At the time of his death a house on Deeside had been built and furnished for him though he never lived to make use of it.

By 1867 the Highlander was firmly established in an unassailable position; he had made himself indispensable to the Queen. Bereft of her husband as she was and living in seclusion a man was needed for those small services which no member of the Household could, by his very position, perform. As her personal attendant Brown could, and did, arrange rugs and shawls for her comfort; he expressed himself with a blunt familiarity which the Queen accepted indulgently and in terms which no one even among her own family would have dared to use. He addressed

*Queen Victoria with Princess Louise, John Brown and the dog, Sharp, Osborne, 1868*

her as 'Wumman', laced her tea with whisky and often, when driving the Queen abroad, would ostentatiously interpose himself between the Queen and the view, staring ahead with stern disapproval. Tact was not his strong point; he spoke rudely to visiting officials; he fished and shot on the estates as he thought fit; rode – with the Queen's permission – her ponies when they were denied to other members of the Household. On more than one occasion he was too drunk to perform his duties; the Queen forgave him.

The situation became impossible. In the face of opposition the Queen's attitude hardened. He was 'invaluable' to her; when arrangements were made to exclude Brown from attendance on the Queen she replied that she would not be dictated to. He was necessary for her comfort, and that should have been good enough for everyone.

The Queen was certainly unwise. Overt favouritism breeds jealousy and hostility. She saw in the manoeuverings of those about her to oust Brown an attempt to force her out of her lonely seclusion. There was no one to whom she would turn for advice. Suspiciously, tenaciously she clung to the man whom she trusted implictly, quite failing to see or to accept the criticism which was increasingly being directed towards both herself and Brown. Cartoons began to appear, a secret marriage with Brown was being openly talked of and the Queen was being spoken of as 'Mrs. John Brown'. The scandal spread to Europe and although apologies were made by editors for the publication of ill-natured and unsubstantiated gossip, it was some time before the uproar subsided.

Perhaps the Queen was too short-sighted to appreciate the effect on her subjects of her own seclusion. She was, in those years following the Prince Consort's death, fast becoming a shadowy figure; it seemed as though she were no longer fulfilling her function as Queen – there were even calls for her abdication. Small wonder, then, that in this twilight existence, she should be out of touch with her subjects. In those years her Royal position was an almost crushing burden. She would carry out her duties as Head of the State, she said, but her people must not expect more from her. She could not understand that to be loved a Monarch must be seen to carry out duties and perform functions; to be esteemed the Queen, the Court and her servants must exhibit an unfailing courtesy to those who came to her. Brown was, *par excellence*, the bearer of messages and his terse responses often evoked anger and indignation. The Mayor of Portsmouth waited on the Queen at Osborne to receive an answer to his request that she would attend a Volunteer Review. Brown brought the message: 'The Queen says sairtainly not!' he announced ungraciously, greatly affronting the visitor.

The question of the Queen's marriage with John Brown was never taken seriously by those who were 'in the know'; he was, quite simply, her favourite servant: spoiled and indulged as he was, he became overbearing and conceited.

But there was perhaps something more. Queen Victoria needed a man in her life to whom she could appeal and on whom she could lean. She found it restful to be guided and dictated to; in his dependability and mastery of the situation she found something akin to Prince Albert's, and this was balm to her. Brown could be relied upon to carry out the Queen's wishes and to make decisions whenever necessary. He organised the gillies' Balls at Balmoral which the Queen always attended, eyeing the revels indulgently.

The most unpleasing aspect of Brown's relationship with the Queen was the arrogance which derived from his position. It jarred upon members of the Royal family, especially the Prince of Wales who, as Brown well knew, was not often on the easiest of terms with his mother. The Prince actually refused to accompany the Queen to Balmoral on one occasion when their relationship was particularly bad, since he knew that Brown, who assumed a special eminence in the Highlands, would render his situation impossible. The military, too, suffered. When General Gardiner, an Equerry, arrived for his period of waiting he enquired after the Queen's health. 'The Queen's very well,' Brown replied. 'It was only the other day that she said to me, "There's that domned old fool General Gardiner coming into waiting, and I know he'll be putting his bloody nose into everything that doesn't concern him."'[2] Such was the influence of Brown that when General M'Neill reprimanded Brown for familiar behaviour, he received the same day a letter from the Queen offering the General a minor command in India. With great tact the General replied that he would of course accede to Her Majesty's wishes, but he would be grateful for a reason for such an appointment so that he could explain to his friends. The matter was never again referred to, but the Queen did not forgive the General and avoided him in the future by arranging that his waitings were never at Osborne or Balmoral.

In the late 1870s Brown's health began to give way. He was a heavy drinker, and he suffered from a recurring swelling of the limbs which was diagnosed as erysipelas. He had put on considerable weight and had deteriorated physically; he was no longer the stalwart, handsome Highlander who had come down to Osborne to serve the Queen fifteen years before. As the years passed the blazing rows gradually dwindled but resentment lingered until his death at Windsor in 1883. The Queen was prostrated; she told Sir Henry Ponsonby that she was utterly crushed: '. . . the strong arm and wise advice, warm heart and cheery original way of saying things and the sympathy in any large or small circumstances – is most cruelly missed.'[3]

In the grounds of the Royal residences cairns and monuments were erected to Brown's memory as they had been to the Prince Consort – at Osborne there is a polished granite seat beside the path beneath the south side of the Terrace. It is one of the few remaining, for after the Queen's death many of these were removed, and King Edward VII is said to have smashed with his own hands a number of plaster statuettes of Brown. As we shall see, it was not long before his place was taken by the Munshi.

The last word may perhaps be left in the safe hands of Sir Henry Ponsonby. The Queen's Private Secretary had a soft spot for Brown; in his quiet way he enjoyed the Highlander's rough humour and called him 'a child of nature'. He wrote a few weeks after Brown's death: 'He was the only person who could fight and make the Queen do what she did not wish. He did not always succeed nor was his advice always the best. But I believe he was honest, and with all his want of education, his roughness, his prejudices and other faults he was undoubtedly a most excellent servant to her.'[4]

## 10

# The Prince of Wales at Osborne

If the Prince of Wales was never entirely at his ease when at Osborne, it is certainly not to be wondered at. In the first place happy childhood memories were subdued by his recollections of a sense of inferiority and under-achievement, to say nothing of chastisement, which lasted well into adolescence. There was also the feeling of awe in his mother's presence: Queen Victoria had long been aware that she found difficulty in creating a warm and intimate confidence with her older children and, as the Prince entered into manhood and a more independent way of life, with his own establishment and household, her attitudes towards her eldest son varied between maternal affection and cold, critical disapproval. It is related that when one evening the Prince arrived late at Osborne, he took shelter behind a pillar, mopping the perspiration from his brow, until he could summon up courage to enter the Drawing-Room and pay his respects to his mother.

There were, of course, two sides to the question. Queen Victoria could not entirely forget the episode at the Curragh Camp in 1861, and again, in 1870, when the Prince had been called as a witness in the Mordaunt divorce case and had been obliged to state publicly that there had never been any 'improper familiarity' between himself and Lady Mordaunt (who was by then in a lunatic asylum), she advised him to be more circumspect in future, deploring his association with the 'frivolous, selfish and pleasure-seeking' members of Society in his circle. On the other hand the Prince's public duties, though numerous, were not onerous, and left him with abundant leisure. When he repeatedly sought some field of responsibility in the affairs of state, the Queen peremptorily refused, adding – with some truth initially, perhaps – that he was too indiscreet to be trusted. To this must be added the Prince's distaste for the Queen's quiet and secluded way of life, and his overt dislike of John Brown, her Highland servant, who showed him scant respect and referred to the Queen as 'your mother'. In consequence he rarely visited Balmoral and, when the Court was at Osborne, he tended to live on board his yacht in Cowes Roads, especially during the well-established yachting Week.

By 1871 the Queen's almost total withdrawal from public life, and the extravagant and easy mode of living of the Prince of Wales, had put the Monarchy in some danger. The Prince had been booed in the streets on his return from the Mordaunt case, and there was even talk of a Republic. The Queen, in poor health and in a low nervous state, was distressed by the criticism, but she felt herself unable to undertake more than she was already doing, transacting the business of state from her writing-desk. But in the late autumn public hostility underwent a marked change. The Prince, then at Sandringham, became seriously ill: he had contracted typhoid fever whilst staying at Londesborough Lodge, near Scarborough, where another guest and the Prince's own groom both died from the outbreak. For a time it was feared that illness might be equally fatal to the Prince himself. As the fever took its course he became delirious, proposing reforms which made his listeners' hair stand on end. The Queen hurried from Balmoral to be near him and at one point was told that he was not expected to survive the night. On 14 December, the anniversary of the death of the Prince Consort – from typhoid, it will be remembered – the crisis was reached and the fever abated. The Prince's children, accompanied by the boys' tutor, had been sent to Osborne, where the Queen arrived to spend Christmas as usual, once she was assured of her son's safety.

Early in 1872 the Prince of Wales came to Osborne. The trials of the previous year had left their mark. The Queen, worn down by worry and ill health, had lost two stone in weight and was 'much changed'. On her part she noticed the alteration in her son: she wrote to the Princess Royal that he was 'quite himself again, only gentler and kinder than ever; and there is something different which I can't exactly express. It is like a new life – all the trees and flowers give him pleasure, as they never used to do, and he was quite pathetic over his small wheelbarrow and little tools at the Swiss cottage. He is constantly with Alix, and they seem hardly ever apart!!!!'[1]

The family spent all February at Osborne. In a month when the house could be as cold and cheerless as a well there was a warmth of spirits which comes from momentous relief. When the suggestion came that there should be a Thanksgiving Service to celebrate the Prince's recovery, the Queen hesitated. At first the very idea seemed unthinkable. Characteristically, when she did accept it, she asked that the arrangements should be such that she could be *seen* by the people. It was a decision that required some courage, but in the event the effort was justified. The grave anxiety which had hovered over the nation during the Prince's illness dispelled the wave of unpopularity which had lapped about the Throne. A month of convalescence at Osborne had done them both good, and the cries of Republicanism were drowned in the tumultuous cheers which greeted the Queen and her son as they drove through London from St. Paul's Cathedral. It was the most extraordinary demonstration of loyalty hitherto witnessed in the City: the Monarchy was safe.

11

# Visitors

Visitors to Her Majesty were received at Osborne with the ceremony due to their rank. If they were coming from the mainland
they might be met at Portsmouth or Southampton by one of the
Royal Yachts and, having crossed the Solent, would be transferred to a waiting carriage at Trinity Pier. Royalty would be
met by a member of the family; informally, simply with carriages
for the suite in attendance, but flags and bunting were displayed
at the least excuse and the townsfolk of Cowes always welcomed
an opportunity to demonstrate their loyalty, and the streets
seethed with people when members of the Royal family were
expected.

After briskly ascending the long hill out of the town carriages
entered the grounds of Osborne by the Queen's Gate at the
corner of York Avenue. This gate is opened now only for visits by
the Royal family but was then guarded by police at the Lodge.
The drive, which has never been resurfaced since the Queen's
last journey down it, bends to the right and runs between long
rows of sombre ilexes until it opens out in front of the forecourt
of the Pavilion. The carriages drew up within the glass-enclosed
*porte-cochère* and the occupants were assisted down by footmen
in scarlet coats. The Royal visitor would be met by the Queen
perhaps just inside the door or in the Hall. Towards the end of
her reign, however, the Queen would receive her family in her
sitting-room, whither they would be conducted by a senior
member of the Household.

Lesser mortals alighted from their carriages at the door on
the right of the forecourt. They were greeted by an Equerry or
one of the Queen's ladies – and by the motto 'SALVE' worked
in terra-cotta tiles on the floor of the Corridor, a cheerless passage with its white, ice-cold statues and dimly-gleaming bronzes,
and less than welcoming. They would be conducted to the

Drawing-Room, or for a formal audience, to the Small Drawing-Room adjacent to the Council Room in the Main Wing.
They were sometimes led upstairs to await the Queen in Prince
Albert's Study and Dressing-Room where, looking rather incon-
gruous in a corner, stood a large basin and ewer among the
*bric-à-brac.*

If the visitor had already previously been presented to the
Queen, all that was necessary was a formal bow when she appeared, but it would still be in order to kneel and kiss the Royal
hand. Many were already somewhat awestruck by the ceremony
attending their arrival and the presence of the Queen might
render them inarticulate. The complete self-possession of the
Queen ever since her Accession had commanded the admiration
even of experienced courtiers; visitors were impressed by her
diminutive size – the sweetness of her voice – her expressive face,
and often had difficulty in recalling the details of their first audience. The poet Tennyson, who lived on the Isle of Wight, was
commanded to visit her in the early days of her widowhood, and
was so moved by the experience that 'he could not give a very
connected account of it afterwards . . . It seems that he was
standing with his back to the fire when the Queen entered and
that she came and stood about five paces from him with her arms
crossed, very pale and like a little statue in her self-possession.
She spoke in a quiet, sweet, sad voice and looked very pretty,
with a stately innocence about her, different from other
women.'[1]

The Queen's friendship with her Poet Laureate ripened: a
year later he was asked to bring his wife, Emily, and two sons to
visit her. After touring the grounds with Lady Augusta Bruce
and visiting the Swiss Cottage they returned to the House.

> Soon after we return Lady Augusta is sent for and she comes
> to fetch us to the Queen. We wait in the Drawing-Room and
> after a very little time we heard a quiet shy opening of the door
> and the Queen came in and I kissed her hand. She shook hands
> with the boys and made a very low reverence to A(lfred). All
> the Princesses came in by turns, Prince Leopold also . . . We
> talked of all things in heaven and earth it seemed to me. I
> never met a Lady with whom I could talk so easily and never
> felt so little shy with any stranger after the first few minutes.
> Princess Alice joined pleasantly in the conversation and

Prince Leopold and Lady Augusta talked with the boys . . .
One feels that the Queen is a woman to live and die for . . . I
am sorry that A. might not have a warm shake of the hand
such as the boys and myself had when the Queen retired . . .'[2]

Almost exactly twenty years afterwards Tennyson again
visited the Queen at Osborne. The intervening period had been
marked by increasingly cordial correspondence between them
and another meeting at Windsor. The Queen wrote: 'After
luncheon saw the great Poet Tennyson in dearest Albert's room
for nearly an hour; and most interesting it was. He is grown very
old – his eyesight much impaired and he is very shaky in his legs.
But he was very kind. Asked him to sit down. He talked of the
many friends he had lost and what it would be if he did not feel
and know that there was another world, where there would be no
partings . . . When I took leave of him I thanked him for his
kindness and said I needed it, for I had gone through so much –
and he said you are so alone on that "terrible height, it is Terrible. I've only a year or two to live but I'll be happy to do anything for you I can. Send for me whenever you like." I thanked
him warmly.'[3]

It was an indication of her attachment to Tennyson that the
Queen asked him to sit down, for visitors usually remained
standing in the Queen's presence. Gladstone, though older than
Tennyson (who was then seventy-four and lived on for another
nine years) and far more 'shaky', was never asked to sit. Disraeli,
on the other hand, was invited to do so, though he was much
younger – on the first occasion he thought it more gracious to
decline.

Naturally enough, an interview was closed by the Queen who
retired to her own room, when the visitor was taken to a carriage
by a member of the Household in waiting. The visit of the
Tennyson family was leisurely enough. After they had seen the
Queen they were given tea and taken to a balcony overlooking
the forecourt to see the Queen, Princess Alice, Prince Leopold
and Lady Augusta set off for Newport. They were then taken on
to the Terrace to see the grounds.

There can be no doubt that the almost mystical aura surrounding the Queen which so deeply impressed itself on her visitors was greatly enhanced by the dignity which accompanied her
appearances in public. Gone were the chaotic scenes which had

Above: *Prince Albert's room, 1873.* Below: *The Queen's bedroom, 1873. Wreath, deathbed photograph of the Prince Consort and watch-pocket over his pillow*

marked her Coronation, when medals were scattered wholesale among the peers who scrambled for them like schoolboys. The Queen was well served; Prince Albert had done his work of refurbishing the image of Royalty with great efficiency and the meticulous planning of the Household for every detail of the Queen's life served as a model for other Royal Houses throughout Europe.

12

# 1878 – An Eventful Year

If 1878 seemed an eventful year it was also by no means untypical of so many during the Queen's long widowhood; it was packed with incident, both political and domestic, and filled with happiness and heartache. It was noticeable that at about this time the Queen was moving away from the improving, educative influence of the Prince Consort. Perhaps she was at last beginning to content herself with her own intellectual limitations; her reading became lighter and where there was no precedent to follow her own commonsense came to her rescue – along with her by now very considerable experience: she was dealing with affairs which Albert had not had time to envisage; a grown-up family brought situations and problems which she only could resolve by using her own judgment, without reference to 'what Albert would have wished'.

At the beginning of the year the Queen used a telephone for the first time:

> *January 14, 1878.* After dinner we went to the Council Room [at Osborne] and saw the telephone. A Professor Bell explained the whole process which is most extraordinary. It had been put in communication with Osborne Cottage and we talked with Sir Thomas and Mary Biddulph, also heard some singing quite plainly. But it is rather faint and one must hold the tube rather close to one's ear.[1]

'Most extraordinary' was often the Queen's way of expressing the working of a process which she did not understand. In those days of rapid technological advance there were many inventions, especially those involving electricity, which seemed 'extraordinary'.

In March her beloved son, Prince Arthur, became engaged to

Princess Louise Margaret, a daughter of estranged parents in the
Prussian Royal family. The Queen was at first indignant; Arthur
was too good to marry; it was not a great match: 'It was a great
shock', she wrote. Then her humane feelings predominated: she
was a nice girl, and it was typical of Arthur to wish to give happiness to a child whose home life was so miserable.

Towards the end of July the Queen returned to Osborne. On
the 22nd she received the Prime Minister, Disraeli, Lord Bea-
consfield, in the small Audience Room adjacent to the Council
Room, and conferred on him the Order of the Garter. It was as
much a reward for his warm relationship with her as it was for
his negotiation of her title 'Empress of India', for the Government's purchase of a large number of the Suez Canal Company
shares, and for achieving 'peace with honour' at the Berlin con-
ference.

On August 13 the Queen embarked in the *Victoria and Albert*
at Osborne Bay to review her fleet at Spithead. In overcast and
squally conditions the paddle-driven yacht steamed between the
long lines of warships, their ensigns whipping in the stiff breeze,
and the scene must have reminded her of the review she had
attended with Albert almost exactly twenty-five years previously.
A few days later the Admirals and Captains participating in
the review dined with her at Osborne. Just a week before the review she had managed to find time to drive over to Sandown Bay
on the other side of the Island to see the beached wreck of the
*Eurydice* which had capsized and sunk off the headland that
March.

On August 16 Princess Alice, Grand Duchess of Hesse-
Darmstadt, and her family arrived at Osborne on a four-day
visit. The Queen was delighted to have her daughter with her
once more, but it was all too short. On the 19th they paid a visit
to the King and Queen of Denmark who were taking a holiday at
West Cowes and the following day she left Osborne never to
return. Meanwhile preparations were in hand for Prince
Arthur's wedding.

On November 8 Princess Victoria, Princess Alice's eldest
daughter, was taken ill with diphtheria which spread rapidly
through the family. One by one they recovered:

*Darmstadt. November 15.* 'My precious May no better; suf-
fers so much. I am in such horrible fear. Irene and Ernie fever
less. Ernie's throat very swelled. Louis no worse; almost no spots.

Alicky recovering.'[2]

On November 16 Princess May, her four year old daughter, died – a terrible blow to the gentle, rather fragile woman whose life was devoted to good causes. On December 8 the Grand Duchess herself caught the infection. It is likely that Prince Ernest transmitted the disease to his mother, for when she had broken to him the news of his sister's death, she had tried to comfort him and had kissed him, despite the doctors' instructions. Disraeli, on breaking the news to Parliament, was to call it 'the kiss of death'.

By this time Queen Victoria was at Windsor, where she always went to remember Prince Albert's death. The distraught Queen wandered about full of anxiety for her daughter; and then, by a terrible irony, on the very day itself, exactly four weeks after the death of her daughter and seventeen years after that of her father, Princess Alice died.

The death of the Princess was a milestone in the Queen's life. For twenty years she had been deprived of Vicky's company but the family, however scattered about Europe it might be, was still complete. She had been so proud of her nine, and now there were but eight. Before the year was out another daughter seemed to be lost to her. Princess Louise was to go to Canada with her husband, the Marquess of Lorne, who had been appointed Governor-General. Only two of her children now remained close at hand, Beatrice, and Helena who lived with her husband at Cumberland Lodge, Windsor Great Park. She felt very much alone and Christmas at Osborne was a sombre festival that year.

## The Wedding of Princess Beatrice

Osborne was the scene of another wedding reception in 1885, very different from the one over twenty years earlier when the Queen had been in deep mourning for Prince Albert. This time it was the turn of her last unmarried, and youngest, child, Princess Beatrice, her mother's much loved and constant companion. Her match with Prince Henry of Battenberg was not unexpected: the couple had met at Darmstadt on the occasion of the marriage of his brother, Prince Louis, with Princess Victoria, a grand-daughter of the Queen's. Although the Queen had viewed the young couple with an indulgent eye on the earlier occasion, when it came to the point she cordially detested the idea of their marriage. Marriage was a forbidden topic at the family table and the Queen shied away from the first unwelcome indications that the Princess was in love. Sadly, it was a clear manifestation of the Queen's selfishness: she had long declared that her daughter was indispensable to her. Still, she had nothing against Prince Henry, though the marriage was not popular in Germany and Russia, and it was not long before she capitulated with good grace, having reached an admirable compromise with her daughter. She wrote: 'Prince Henry can therefore understand that it would have been *quite out of the question* for Beatrice ever to leave the Queen, and she would never have wished it herself, knowing well how *impossible* it was for her to leave her Mother. . . . The Prince is, however, ready to make England his home, and the Princess will continue to live with the Queen as heretofore. He is very amiable, very unassuming and sensible, and in addition, very good-looking.'[1]

It is not every young bridegroom who would willingly forgo his independence and, without even setting up his own estab-lishment, agree to live with his mother-in-law. But the Prince also possessed the quality of compliance in addition to those remarked by the Queen: he recognised that there was no alternative for the two of them and with good grace he set out to succeed in his unusual role.

The wedding took place on July 23, at one in the afternoon. It was a glorious day and Prince Henry was quick to note the scale of the preparations. Accommodation was strictly limited: the houses on the Osborne estate were packed, as were the hotels in the district, and the Royal yachts, anchored in Osborne Bay, were also called upon. The situation was complicated of course by the swarms of servants brought to attend upon the guests themselves. The Lord Chamberlain's department took the full brunt of the arrangements, though the Household at Osborne were necessarily concerned with much of the local detail. St. Mildred's, Whippingham, was luxuriantly decorated for the occasion; a covered way with tiers of seats on either side was erected between the churchyard gate and the porch; the organist and the choristers of St. George's Chapel, Windsor, were summoned to augment the somewhat limited resources of the small Island parish: unhappily, records show that the choirboys could not be provided with refreshment, such was the pressure upon the catering department: perhaps Mr. Parratt, the organist, arranged something suitable for them.

The Queen ordained, rather vaguely, that 'demi-toilette' should be worn: eventually more explicit instructions were issued. Ladies were to wear long dresses with sleeves to the elbow. Jewels were to be worn as for a formal evening party. Those who would travel down for the occasion and return the same day got off more lightly: they might wear bonnets and smart morning dresses – which of course were then long.

Prince Henry arrived on 20 July, accompanied by his family. At a private investiture he received the Order of the Garter and the Queen conferred upon him the title of Royal Highness. He arrived at the church supported by his two brothers, Alexander, Prince of Bulgaria and Prince Francis Joseph of Battenberg, and wearing the glittering white uniform of the 'Gardes du Corps', crossed with the blue ribbon of the Garter. A Guard of Honour of Princess Louise's Argyll and Sutherland Highlanders was mounted in front of Whippingham Church and, at the other end of the bridal route, a similar Guard of Honour of the Isle of Wight Volunteers at the Queen's Gate, Osborne.

Princess Beatrice was happy and composed. She wore a wedding dress of white satin trimmed with orange blossom and lace, with lace on the neckline and sleeves. The Queen, as a mark of unique generosity to her favourite daughter, lent her the Honiton lace she had worn at her own wedding with Prince Albert, and which was one of her most treasured possessions. The Princess, like the ten bridesmaids who waited upon her, carried a bouquet of orange blossom.

Along the route carriages had been parked in neighbouring fields, for the whole Island was *en fête*, and all along the winding lanes crowds waved and cheered, and there was a burst of applause when the carriage procession approached the churchyard gate. The Princess moved up the aisle with the Queen on her left and the Prince of Wales on her right and the marriage service commenced, conducted by the Archbishop of Canterbury assisted by the Dean of Windsor and Canon Prothero, Rector of Whippingham. When it had all ended the procession reformed to return to Osborne. We can picture it all: the carriages rumbling along the road, past the Guard of Honour and up the final stretch of drive beyond the Queen's Gate, now so neglected, to draw up at the porch of the Pavilion Wing, after which the spectators retired from their vantage points among the flowering hedgerows well content with their glimpse of a splendour unparalleled on the Island. Indoors, in the Antler Room, the Register was signed by no fewer than forty-four persons, beginning with the Queen and ending with Canon Prothero. The guests crowded the wide lawns, lunching in two large tents, while military bands played throughout the afternoon. The Queen, with the bride and groom and close relatives, lunched indoors.

At five o'clock the bridal couple drove off for their honeymoon at nearby Quarr Abbey. As honeymoons go it was short – only two days, and even this the Queen regretted: honeymoons seemed to her an unnecessary institution, especially when they meant she was left alone. But their departure had no effect upon the festivities: perhaps there had never been a party anything like this at Osborne, and certainly there never would be again. Guests returning the same day left shortly after the couple to travel to London by carriage, Royal Yacht and special train. *The Illustrated London News* reported: 'The view from the North Front of the brilliantly illuminated palace was very beautiful. As the Royal and noble guests wandered in and out among the bronze statues, the air was sweet with the odour of the flower-beds and fresh with the scent of the neighbouring sea. In the centre of the great lawn rose a fountain hung with many-coloured lamps, and countless glow-worms of light were festooned from stanchions between the fountains. The sounds of laughter made pleasant echoes in the night, and strains of music from the bands mingled with the distant splash of oars plying the sea. Upon the Guardship (H.M.S. *Exeter*), the Queen's yachts and a couple of gunboats, the fireworks gleamed and paled, and died out in the darkness . . .'[2]

The Queen and the Royal family dined out in the marquees. The Duke of Cambridge observed that she was looking wonderfully cheerful and well: she had reason to be, for events proved that she had by no means lost a daughter and had indeed gained a son. She had recorded her misgivings before the wedding, expressing them somewhat ambiguously: '. . . the Wedding Day is the great trial – but I hope and pray there may be no result! That would aggravate everything and besides make me terribly anxious.'[3] But the day was a matter for triumph: in the solitude of her sitting-room, while the guests were still celebrating and her tenants were enjoying their own Ball, she wrote: 'A happier looking couple could seldom be seen kneeling at the altar together. It was very touching. I stood very close to my dear child, who looked very sweet, pure and calm . . . When the Blessing had been given I tenderly embraced my darling "Baby".'[4] The result, whatever Queen Victoria meant, were the four Battenberg children, who gave her great happiness in the last years of her life.

After that mere apology for a honeymoon the couple returned to Osborne to take up residence with the Queen. Prince Henry's role was by no means an easy one but he quietly and unostentatiously, though firmly, found a place for himself in the Royal circle. His wife, now Princess Henry of Battenberg, occupied the position of companion and support to her mother as she had throughout her adult life, for it had never been suggested that she would simply relinquish her duties on marriage. Clearly, Prince Henry would have to forgo that independence of status that marriage ordinarily confers upon a man: he had no home of his own in which to be master, neither could the couple adopt their own routine. Instead they moved and lived in the Queen's well-worn ways, subject always to the demands of an exacting, if affectionate, mistress.

But marriage brought new opportunities for the Princess, and in a widening public life she was often accompanied by her husband. Despite his youth and the aging Queen's preference for the company of her own contemporaries, the Prince contrived to infuse a new spirit into Court life. He was a keen sportsman, playing golf and tennis at Osborne, sailing the waters of the Solent and even as far as the Mediterranean in his fine schooner, the *Sheilagh*, a gift from the Queen. The Princess was no less keen a sailor and the pair spent a good deal of time on board together. At Balmoral he was a keen shot, and still found time to sail about the West coast of Scotland. He took a leading part in those amateur dramatics and tableaux which the Queen so greatly enjoyed: above all, his happiness was infectious; visitors found that the heaviness of Osborne had been lifted and replaced by a lightness and gaiety that had not been felt for many years. They rejoiced in their children and, despite the difficulties, the marriage was a happy one: it was, however, to have a tragic sequel.

## Queen Victoria and the Munshi

The sitting-room at Osborne was the scene of one of the Queen's increasingly rare, but still formidable rages. It concerned the Munshi.

In 1887, the Queen received into her Household two Indian servants, or Khitmagars. Abdul Karim was a clever and ambitious young Moslem who caught the Queen's fancy and was soon promoted to be Munshi (teacher). His rapid rise to favour caused jealousy and suspicion among the Royal Household and especially his Indian fellow-servants. In particular, hostility was aroused by the Munshi's advancement of a Moslem friend, Rafiuddin Ahmed, who was believed to be in touch with elements in India which were keen to rebel against the British Raj. It appeared to the Household that Queen Victoria's confidence in the Munshi, from whom she was now learning a little Hindustani, had induced her to show him despatches from India. The Munshi himself was boasting that his father was a Surgeon-General, and the courtiers anxiously sought information from India about his background. It was then that 'Fritz' Ponsonby, about to join the Household as a junior Equerry, was asked by the Queen to seek out the Munshi's father, and find out about him. Ponsonby discovered the father at Agra, where he was not, as claimed, a Surgeon-General, but an apothecary at the town jail. Ponsonby's report was not well received by the Queen, who showed her displeasure by not inviting him to dinner for over a year. This was a powerful snub, since it was the Queen's custom to invite her courtiers to dine with her fairly regularly.

The Queen persisted in showing her complete confidence in the Munshi, however, and sought further advice. Prince Louis of Battenberg, the father of Earl Mountbatten of Burma, came to Osborne and suggested tactfully that the idea of a Moslem seeing the Queen's confidential papers would be greatly resented by the Hindus, and would also cause offence to the Indian Princes, who

Above: *The Queen's sitting-room, 1873. Despatch boxes beside writing table.* Below: *Queen Victoria and the Munshi, 1893*

were then in an influential position. This ingenious – and perfectly true – statement caused the Queen to abandon her plans for showing confidential papers to the Munshi, but to show her own trust in him she gave him the title of her 'Indian Secretary'.

The Queen's tenacity in the face of steady opposition is remarkable: indeed, opposition often only steeled her own determination, and when she chose, she could be extraordinarily smallminded. In this case her judgment may be questioned, but another aspect must be considered: her dislike of prejudice and intolerance. In her regard for the Eastern peoples she was ahead of her time. Her dislike of a rigid system of social class was well known; hence in part her obstinacy in her promotion of the Munshi's cause. For two years the wrangle continued, though it seems likely that by this time the Munshi was considered by the Court in general no longer dangerous, but only a nuisance and a bore.

In 1897 matters came to a head. Queen Victoria announced that she would take the Munshi with her on her visit to Cimiez. By the nature of things this would mean that he would now be dining with the Household – and this was not to be tolerated. Harriet Phipps, the Queen's personal secretary, was deputed to break the news to the Queen – she must choose between the Munshi or the Household. Her Majesty exploded with anger, sweeping all the paraphernalia of her crowded desk on to the floor. There seemed no solution to the impasse: the Queen would not be dictated to by the Household; the Household would not associate with the Munshi. Fortunately the Prime Minister, Lord Salisbury, was staying at Osborne. He was summoned and his opinion sought. That astute politician was able to convince her that the French were too 'odd' to understand the Munshi, and might not treat him with proper respect. He advised her to leave him at home: she complied, and everyone's honour was saved.

The attitude of the Household becomes more understandable when we learn that the Munshi nevertheless turned up at Cimiez, unheralded and unbidden and, worse still, accompanied by the politically untrustworthy Ahmed, who was sent swiftly packing. After this the Munshi's influence declined. He continued to serve the Queen, living at Arthur Cottage near the Prince of Wales' Gate at Osborne: there were rumours of wild and sinister parties there, never clearly substantiated. Certainly he was popular among the children on the estate. There are those still living (1977) who can recall with pleasure his parties for them. On the Queen's death the Munshi was obliged to destroy his personal papers relating to her at his Windsor home, Frogmore Cottage. He then retired to Agra, India. His last contact with the Royal family was made in 1905 when the Prince of Wales, later King George V, accepted a visit from him during his tour of India. The Prince wrote to his father: 'He has not grown more beautiful and is getting fat. I must say he was most civil & humble & really pleased to see us . . . I am told he lives quietly (at Karim Lodge) & gives no trouble at all.'[1] He died in 1909.

The tone of these remarks reflects the earlier dislike among courtiers and Royal family in which the Munshi was held. His complacency was a constant source of friction during the Queen's last years. Undoubtedly, Queen Victoria was at fault for promoting the causes of the Munshi and Ahmed against the advice of Ministers and courtiers, and of the Viceroy of India himself. Politically, she should not have favoured a Moslem at a time of increasing religious unrest in India and, equally, her inflexible attitude towards the Household on this question cannot well be justified. But Queen Victoria was loyal to the least of her subjects; in the Isle of Wight and at Balmoral, too, her interest in the well-being of simple, rural folk was sustained throughout her life. Perhaps it was a means of escape from the formality and remoteness of the Court life which she had built round herself like a shell, but it was none the less genuine for that. The affair must also be seen in the light of her Proclamation as Empress of India: since then she had made a surrender to all things Indian. It was not for nothing that when she built an extension to Osborne it should be in the Indian style and taste and named the Durbar Room. If she could not visit India herself, India could – and did – come to Osborne. 'The poor Munshi', as the Queen wrote of him, may have lost a little of his lustre after the Cimiez episode but he remained in close attendance on the Queen and his ubiquitous presence made the Household grind their teeth in impotent exasperation. In July, 1899, Marie Mallet was writing: '. . . I am for ever meeting him in passages or the garden or face to face on the stairs and each time I shudder more . . .'[2] In our reconstruction of life at Osborne, just as any scene of Queen Victoria in the 1870s must include the stalwart, kilted figure of John Brown, so no glimpse of her in the 90s would be complete without the turbaned and swarthy Munshi standing nearby.

## Princess May at Osborne

It was hardly to be expected that in so large a family as Queen Victoria's there were not frequent causes for mourning. For the more distant relatives in Europe the trappings of grief were little more than a formality – 'Here we are, in mourning again,' the Queen once wrote almost lightheartedly. 1861 proved a terrible year, however, with the death of the Queen's mother, the Duchess of Kent and, a few months later, that of the Prince Consort himself. For many years the Queen's morbid horror of death persisted, yet at Osborne she was to be so often the pillar of the family to whom the stricken relatives came for solace and support.

Early in 1892 Prince Albert Victor, Duke of Clarence and Avondale, called 'Eddy' by his family, and eldest son of the Prince of Wales, died at Sandringham House, of complications following influenza. Scarcely a month previously this volatile and unpromising young man, who seemed to live only for pleasure, had become engaged to Princess May of Teck (later to become Queen Mary), and it was hoped that she would bring a stabilising influence into his life. But it was not to be: tragedy struck swiftly. Christmas at Sandringham was a dismal affair in 1891; there was 'flu in the family, several of the party had heavy colds, and Prince George, Eddy's younger brother, was recovering from typhoid. At the beginning of the second week in January Prince Eddy was feverish and ill: he struggled downstairs for his birthday, but was unable to attend the family dinner party. Then pneumonia set in and after a painful struggle he died on the 14 January.

Soon after the funeral the bereaved fiancée came with her parents, the Duke and Duchess of Teck, to Osborne. They travelled to Portsmouth by train and crossed to the Isle of Wight in the *Alberta*. Queen Victoria received them with great kindness;

her heart went out to the poor child. 'The dear girl looks like a
crushed flower, but is resigned and quiet & gentle. She is grown
thinner, but otherwise is not looking ill.'[1]


The Queen had been greatly taken with the Princess since as long
ago as 1884. After a year of mourning and of readjustment to the
idea of Prince George as a future Heir to the throne after his
father, it came as no very great surprise to learn of Princess
May's engagement to him. *The Times* gave authoritative approval to the match: 'The predominant feeling . . . will be that this
betrothal accords with the fitness of things, and, so far from
offending any legitimate sentiment, is the most appropriate and
delicate medicament for a wound in its nature never wholly
effaceable. . .'(May 5,1893).
     Queen Victoria was delighted. She wrote to her grandson:
'. . . how thankful I am that this great and so long & ardently
wished for event is settled & I gladly give my consent to what I
pray may be for your happiness and for the Country's good. . .'[2]
     The marriage was celebrated at St. James's Palace on July 6
and the honeymoon was spent at York Cottage, Sandringham.
At the beginning of August the newly married couple came to
Osborne. The Isle of Wight was *en fête* to receive them, and the
ships in the Roads and harbour were dressed overall with bunting. They had travelled by train from London and, as in that sad
journey only eighteen months previously, had crossed from
Portsmouth in the *Alberta*. They were welcomed at Trinity Pier
by the Prince of Wales, his nephew, the Emperor of Germany,
and other members of the Royal family. York Avenue was gaily
decorated in their honour as the carriage procession took them to
Osborne. There they were received by the Queen herself who was
attended by Princess Louise and the Connaught and Battenberg
grand-children. The Queen wrote: 'Dear Georgie and May had a
vy pretty and hearty reception on Monday evg. – Sailors, flags –
900 schoolchildren – Soldiers fm Trinity Pier almost up the Hill
to the Lodge & our Tenants inside the grounds. The evg. was
bright and fine.'[3] Princess May wrote to her mother:

> After a short talk we were shown our rooms downstairs, under
> those we had last year, & opening on to the pretty terrace. We

each have a sitting & dressing room – After tea I drove with
Grandmamma in the grounds, this place is looking quite
lovely, so fresh & green, & I am quite in love with it. It was a
perfect evening.[4]

So indeed had the weather been all through their engagement
and honeymoon. It had been a brilliant summer, almost suffocat-
ingly hot at times, and must have exhausted Princess May, unac-
customed to being so much in the limelight, but she remained
outwardly unaffected by the ordeal of her entry into this new
public life which she would now henceforth be leading. She was
charming and unassuming and fully confirmed the view that
Queen Victoria had earlier formed of her. 'I cannot say how
much pleased I am & we all are with dear May,' the Queen wrote
at this time. 'She is so unaffected and sensible, & so very dis-
tinguished & dignified in her manner – & vy civil to every one. –
She is vy pretty & the more you see her, the more I like & admire
her . . . I really feel quite happy abt this dear young *ménage* –
whom may God bless and protect.'[5] Thus the elderly Queen
expressed herself, unambiguously, if ungrammatically, and with
high satisfaction at this fulfilment of her hopes.

Certainly, Princess May managed extremely well. It must be
remembered that she was already a member of the Royal family,
being descended through her mother from King George III, and
his son, the Duke of Cambridge, and had not therefore entered
into the company of strangers. However, her role was a new one.
During the Princess's fortnight's stay at Osborne, she found herself moved high in the order of precedence – an indication by the
Queen of what her position now meant. The Princess was
amused at being 'pushed on' by the 'Aunts,' but behaved with
great good sense.

On the evening of the arrival of the Duke and Duchess of York
there was a dinner party for fifty-five in the Durbar Room,
which had been completed only the year before. Its exterior
matched the rest of the House, to which it was adjacent on the
north side of the Pavilion, thus forming a third side to the Forecourt. The interior was decorated in the Oriental taste with
fretted plaster-work and hung with Indian fabrics. Electric light
had been installed, and in general it was much admired as a
symbol of the Queen's interest and affection for her Indian
Empire. 'The Indian Room is magnificent,' Princess May wrote,

'& it was such a pretty sight. I sat next to William (the German Emperor) who made himself most agreeable, Uncle Arthur (the Duke of Connaught) sat on my other side. Fancy me, little me, sitting next to William, the place of honour!!! It seemed so strange. . . . After dinner great presentation of German suite & others, military, naval, etc. I talked my best German. We got away at 11.30.'[6]

All the honours of Osborne were conferred upon the Princess. She breakfasted in a tent on the lawn with the Queen, who was fully attended by her Indian servants, and whose breakfast service, except for cup and saucer, was of solid gold. She visited the Prince and Princess of Wales, who were on the *Osborne* for Cowes Week: the ladies all wore yachting caps and white dresses. There was an atmosphere of serene and civilised luxury, ease and wealth seldom encountered elsewhere on such a scale. It must be remembered that at that time the English nobility was secure; it had passed unscathed through the year of revolutions which rocked other European nations.

It was an unforgettable fortnight for the new Duchess of York. She was constantly out in public, and always there were crowds and welcomes, and cheers; in her quieter moments she gave sittings to Tuxen, the painter, who officially recorded the wedding of the Duke and Duchess in a picture which today hangs in Buckingham Palace. Her Aunt Augusta wrote to Princess May, asking if she were pleased with her reception at Osborne. Indeed she was; she could look out with composure and satisfaction from her window overlooking the terrace across the green lawns and the Italian Garden to the sparkling blue of the Solent, now so often white with sails. She could reflect on her latest outing and sit down and write with becoming modesty to her mother: 'I drove with her (the Queen) to West Cowes where the people wished to see me. The people were most civil.'[7] So were they, and so did they remain throughout those long years when, as Queen Mary, mutual affection bound her to her people.

# Death of Prince Henry

Prince Henry of Battenberg's life combined duty and pleasure but was certainly not full enough for a fit, active man in his thirties; and so it was not to be wondered at that he volunteered to accompany an expeditionary force to Ashanti, where insurrection had broken out. Prince Christian Victor, the Queen's grandson, had been permitted to join the volunteers, and no one was surprised when Prince Henry, his close friend and relative by marriage, wished to do likewise. His ancestry had led certain sections of the British Press and public to regard him as a German intruder who, in those days when Anglo-German rivalry was developing, was far too close to the Queen's ear. In his application to the Queen Prince Henry wrote that he hoped by this act of service to prove his loyalty to the country he had adopted. Nevertheless, the Queen would not entertain the idea; the whole thing was out of the question. At this point Princess Beatrice entered the arena. She was not insensitive to her husband's enforced inactivity and perceived that he felt deeply the comparison to be drawn between his own life and that of his active brothers. The Queen hesitated, then finally capitulated. 'Liko' might go – though she dreaded the dangers of fever.

Early in December, 1895, the expedition left England. On the 27th the main column landed and set off on the march to Kumasi, the centre of the rebel King Prempeh. On 10 January, 1896, while still forty miles from their goal, Prince Henry was struck down with malaria. Dangerously ill, he was carried back to the coast where he embarked on H.M.S. *Blonde*, which at once sailed for England. Three days later the Prince was dead, ironically on the very day that the rebels submitted to the British force.

At Osborne the news of the Prince's death came as a terrible shock. True, there had been reports of fever but not such as to give rise to anxiety. It had even been suggested that the Princess might join her husband at Madeira. When she read the telegram announcing that the happiness of ten years was over, there seemed little left for her to live for. 'The life is gone out of me,' she said.

Meanwhile Prince Henry's body was on the way home. In order to preserve it in the fierce heat of the tropics it was placed in a coffin made of biscuit tins and immersed, not like Lord Nelson's before him in brandy, but in rum. At Madeira the coffin was transferred to H.M.S. *Blenheim* which arrived in England on 4 February.

Princess Beatrice, accompanied by her brothers the Prince of Wales and Prince Arthur, Duke of Connaught; her sister Helena, Princess Christian, and Princes Louis and Francis of Battenberg sailed in the *Alberta* to Portsmouth where the *Blenheim* was berthed. There, in the Captain's cabin, a short service was held by the coffin, which was then transferred to the *Alberta* for passage to Trinity Pier, Cowes. As the ship passed up the Medina River that calm winter's afternoon ship's bells tolled and minute guns crashed their salute to the dead. As the *Alberta* came alongside the Queen drove down from Osborne, bringing with her two of Prince Henry's children, Prince Alexander who was ten and Princess Ena, nine. The coffin lay amidships on the upper deck and there the Queen laid her wreath among the banks of flowers.

The funeral at Whippingham took place the next day. Early that morning Princess Beatrice left Osborne with her children to make a private farewell to her husband. Later, the procession set out from the House, with the Princess in the Queen's carriage: the Prince's coffin, mounted on a gun-carriage, rumbled along those roads which ten years earlier had echoed to happy greetings, and which were now silent and lined with troops. Only too well did the old Queen share her daughter's emotions as they sat there together, deeply veiled in black, and only too clearly did she remember her premonitions of fever. That she had, in the result, been proved right was no consolation to her.

Two unexpected consequences followed upon Prince Henry's death. The first was the reaction of the public. Members of the Expedition to Ashanti were pressed for details of the Prince when they arrived back in England, and the public learned with surprise of his cheerfulness: how, in his capacity of Military Secretary to the leader, Sir Francis Scott, he had impressed native chiefs who heard with awe that he was the husband of a daughter of the Queen herself: With tragic irony the tide of opinion swung in his favour: he had indeed 'proved his devotion to his adopted country', and proved it to the hilt.

The second was just as unexpected and something more of a shock to the Queen. Both she and the Princess had been at the same age when they had lost their husbands: the Queen had gone into retirement after Prince Albert's death: now the Princess was to take her children to France for a month, leaving her mother alone. It was a remarkable test of character in one who had been brought up to be the Queen's constant companion but it was, she felt, the only way in which she could re-create a family life. A week after the funeral she said goodbye and departed, leaving alone at Osborne a grief-stricken old lady, utterly forlorn. A few days later, just before she left for Windsor, the Queen went out in an open carriage for her usual drive accompanied by her Lady-in-Waiting, then Lady Errol. Princess Marie Louise recalled the occasion:

> The Queen was very silent, and Leila (Lady Errol) thought it was time to make a little conversation. So she said; 'Oh, Your Majesty, think of when we shall see our dear ones again in Heaven!'
> 'Yes,' said the Queen.
> 'We will all meet in Abraham's bosom,' said Leila.
> 'I will *not* meet Abraham,' said the Queen, who afterwards wrote in her diary: 'Dear Leila, not at all consolatory in moments of trouble!'[1]

The Princess's experiment was not wholly successful: memories of her husband inhabited every one of the Queen's homes, and when she returned to resume her post by her mother's side, they became almost unendurable. Certainly, though, the Queen loved her Battenberg grand-children. At Osborne they learned to ride and swim: Princess Ena was a lovely and affectionate child and the boys were active and intelligent. Gradually, the warmth of family life was infused once more into the great house.

★

Prince Henry's funeral did not, however, quite mark the end

of the whole tragic affair. In 1898 the *Blonde* returned to England and Victorian sentiment demanded a poignant visit to the scene of the Prince's death. Marie Mallet, a Lady-in-Waiting, wrote:

> *Osborne, July 22nd, 1898.*
> We have just returned from visiting the *Blonde*. The Queen wished us all to see where Prince Henry died and the Captain seemed to take a melancholy pride in the whole sad story and gave us many details. Altogether it was mournful and depressing; even the sight of Lady Errol in jetted cape and plumed bonnet squeezing herself into the conning tower failed to raise our spirits.[2]

> *July 24th, 1898.*
> . . . In the morning I went on board the *Alberta* with the Queen and Princesses and we steamed as near as possible to the *Blonde* and anchored close to her in Osborne Bay in order that the Officers and Petty Officers who were on board at the time of Prince Henry's death might come on board and be presented. The Captain also brought his dog, a spaniel; thanks to a strict diet of ship's biscuit and salad oil this animal not only survived three years of West Africa, it flourished. Poor beast, it appears it took an immense fancy to Prince Henry and never left his side for a moment . . . Poor Princess Beatrice, it was her wedding day (the 23rd), and therefore doubly trying, but although her eyes were red and swollen she took photographs of the vessel and talked as cheerfully as though life was beginning instead of ending for her. She must have *no* imagination, that is the only explanation I can offer.[3]

Perhaps it was sheer courage: the widowed Princess had spent her own childhood in a house of mourning, with a widowed Queen, secluded and remote from most other children and from normal social intercourse. She had witnessed at first hand, and at an impressionable age, the effects of deep and prolonged grief, and she perhaps felt that surrender to it might endanger her sense of proportion with her own young family and her attention to duty. Marie Mallet was but very recently married and it might well have seemed inconceivable to her that anyone could undergo so harrowing an experience apparently unmoved.

Prince Henry's death came as a severe shock to the Queen: at thirty-eight he had been the one young man at Court who was acceptable to her. Characteristically, Princess May summed up the situation:

> 'Isn't it sad about poor Liko?' she wrote. 'Poor Aunt Beatrice it is awful for her, her whole life ruined, one's heart bleeds for her in her fearful sorrow – What will the Queen and she do now, those 2 women quite alone, it is too sad and depressing to think of.'[4]

Early in February Princess May's mother arrived at Osborne to find the Queen and her daughter in tears and deeply upset by some thoughtless and unkind words expressed by Princess Louise. The whole atmosphere at Osborne reverted to deep mourning, from which, despite family parties and reunions with grandchildren, it perhaps never really recovered.

## 17

# Queen Victoria at Work

Memories of Osborne, whether of family life and the bustle of movement or of Privy Councils held in a sepulchral hush, must always be dominated by the scene of a tiny, bonneted figure sitting at a table writing. In the Queen's private sitting room the two tables, side by side, form the central feature and epitomise her working life.

To the end of her reign she was a conscientious, industrious and prolific writer. As a little girl she had remarked; 'I hate idleness'.

*Osborne, the drawing-room, 1885.* (Photo H. N. King)

Her letters to her daughter in Prussia fill volumes; to these must be added others to the rest of her large family, to Ministers of State and to her Household. Letters, minutes, memoranda, brief notes, all poured from her pen. Small wonder, then, that her handwriting tended to race across the page; crossings out were frequent and the punctuation was guided more by the need to express herself than by any clear rule. Yet she had the gift of making herself understood; by the use of underlining words and whole phrases sometimes two or three times she transmitted unambiguously the force of her feelings. She had a tendency sometimes to telescope ideas together to form a single yet comprehensive image as we see in her letter to the Princess Royal quoted after the title page. Added to all this she found time to keep a Journal, to write two volumes of *Leaves from a Journal of Our Life in the Highlands*, to write to *The Times* and, when occasion demanded, to draft Court Circulars, as she did on the death of her servant, John Brown.

The Queen's last illness revealed all her astonishing industry. When she was no longer able to conduct State business the despatch boxes which arrived by every boat piled up with alarming rapidity. No one had really appreciated before, though messengers came and went daily, just how much work the Queen achieved in a day, though her sight had long been failing. In fine weather she would sit out under a tent on the lawn, or she would write from the Lower Alcove, a small, semi-circular, shell-lined grotto on the lower terrace; or from the Upper Alcove from which she could look down the valley to the sea. Someone was always in attendance, a Lady-in-Waiting, John Brown, the Munshi, Princess Beatrice. Sometimes she would sit out under the trees, behind a round table covered with a tasselled cloth. She wrote on paper which was thickly edged with black after the Prince Consort's death, and on which was an engraving of Osborne House or the Royal Cypher.

The silence might be oppressive indoors, where her courtiers worked and awaited her summons; but outside, in the summer, the air was full of the sound of birds and the murmur of the sea; carriages rumbled up the sombre drive and along the road; it was all very quiet however, especially in the Queen's later years. All this, the great House, the Court, the Royal yachts busy on their errands across Spithead, all centred on the small, dumpy, rather homely figure, writing away along miles of paper. It was a scene that did not change much with the years. In those earlier golden days at Osborne the Prince Consort was often at the Queen's side, perhaps even more industrious, even more deeply absorbed in his work. There was more movement, more noise; the children were at lessons in their rooms upstairs; there was riding instruction, and sketching out of doors: sometimes there was quarrelling on a Royal scale. Into all this the Queen managed to fit yet more, continuing her own lessons from her drawing master, Leitch, contriving to spend time with the children at the Swiss Cottage and on the beach; giving Audiences and bearing more children.

It is difficult adequately to convey the scope of the Queen's interests. She remained aloof from the world of politics but took an interest in social legislation; she threw herself heart and soul into national causes and visited the sick and wounded. Gradually her experience and confidence increased, and the time came when no one could gainsay her with the exception, perhaps, of Mr. Gladstone, whom she cordially disliked. Her literary tastes were simple; she admired Tennyson's poetry; she enjoyed Charlotte Brontë and Dickens and conscientiously worked her way through many of the Victorian novels. Opera and ballet delighted her, and she loved riding, sketching and music. Her tastes had been formed very largely by Prince Albert and tended perhaps towards the Germanic. Winterhalter was her favourite artist and Mendelssohn's was perhaps her best-loved music. She was, as were all her children, bi-lingual in English and German, and possessed a flair for languages. She detested the ways of Society; she launched an attack on the demoralising effect the idle rich had upon her eldest son and, later, upon *his* eldest son, Prince Albert Victor. She looked forward to a levelling of the social classes, but was strangely blind to the sufferings of small children working long hours in industry.

All these interests and many others are reflected in her family letters. Nothing was too trivial to escape her attention and she was able to proceed from State affairs to domestic matters with bewildering rapidity. Through her constant communication with her large European family she contrived to keep herself almost frighteningly well informed. Again and again she would comment on affairs which some member of her family had tried to keep from her, and those who failed became exasperated at the efficiency of her system. 'I ask again, *who* is it tells the Queen these things?'[1] wrote a querulous courtier. It must be remembered that the circle around the Royal family was a close one, members of the Household were often related to one another, or had close ties formed by education or Army service and, by necessity, they were in frequent touch with each other in their service to Royalty. News percolated upwards from level to level, casually and unofficially, until it eventually and unfailingly reached the ears of the Queen.

She worked on until only a week before her death. Only now papers were read aloud to her for comment, amendment and signature. The strong sloping handwriting had at last become fainter and more shaky. She complained to 'Fritz' Ponsonby, her Assistant Secretary, that she could not read his writing, that the light indoors was very bad, that it had been a dismal autumn. There was no help for it; the Queen's eyesight was failing, yet she worked on. It is a measure of her devotion to State papers that any other activity called for comment. Occasionally, a member of the Household would wait on the Queen and discover her busy with some piece of needlework but it was rare that she was thus employed.

The Queen greatly enjoyed her drives and outings which provided a diversion from the endless paperwork. Always the arrangements for the ladies accompanying her were meticulous. Lady Lytton, in waiting at Osborne during August, 1899, describes some of those spacious days:

*15 August.* Lovely hot day arrived at Osborne – nice tea out under the tree. The Connaughts, Princess Christian and Princess Thora made a large merry party. Band in the evening so only spoke to the Queen a few minutes after dinner. Each day was lovely and sitting out under the cedar so very pleasant.

*16 August.* Drove with the Queen and she and Princess Christian talked so cheerfully and happily. The sunset was perfectly beautiful with scarlet red green blue sky and grey cloud effects.

*19 August.* Went with the Queen on board the *Victoria and Albert* and for a nice cruise to the sea and Hurst Castle and saw the Needle rocks and had a good fresh breeze, but it was very hot ... Albani and Rumford sang beautifully in the evening and it is always so luxurious to sit comfortably in a drawing-room with good music.

*23 August.* . . . Mary Hughes and I drove with the Queen by the sea. A man rushed at the carriage and threw in a letter just before the Lodge. A German photographer but it is a grave offence. Last man got two years. Sat by the Queen at dinner but all easy and pleasant.[2]

There were the inevitable, but fortunately rare, intrusions of cranks, lunatics and irresponsible people into the Queen's private life. At such times she was courageous and imperturbable. Disasters, however, evoked an immediate and sympathetic response in her: she was acutely concerned with the sufferings of individuals, especially the bereaved whose feelings she shared. It was often just this concern for others, capricious and unexpected as it might be, that drew people to her and won for her respect and affection.

18

## Last Years

During Queen Victoria's last years her health remained generally good. Rheumatism encroached steadily on her mobility from
1895, compelling her to use first a stick, and later, a wheel-chair.
At Osborne a lift had been installed just off the entrance hall,
and she could thus avoid any sense of confinement. Nearly every
day, apparently impervious to the weather, she would emerge
and enter her carriage by way of a baize-covered plank, attended
by Indian servants, for her knees had been seriously affected by
two falls. Heavily swathed in shawls and snugly wrapped in rugs,
she was driven about the grounds at a snail's pace, accompanied
by Princess Beatrice, a visiting relative or one of her ladies-in-
waiting. Her children had grown up and all but one had left
home: Princess Alice and Prince Leopold were already long
dead; 'Affie' died of cancer of the throat in 1900 – his son,
'young Alfred' had died the year before; 'Vicky' was dying in
agony from spinal cancer in Germany. Grandchildren in plenty
provided a large measure of compensation for the sadness that
must inevitably accompany a long life. Princess Beatrice's
fatherless children, who regarded the Queen's homes as their
own, were a perpetual source of happiness. Moreover, beyond
the immediate confines of home and family, the British people on
the occasion of her Diamond Jubilee in 1897 had shown beyond
question the deep affection in which they held her. On her rare visits
to London crowds thronged Buckingham Palace and cheered
loyally when she appeared at a window. She had become an institution.

From 1898 the Queen's eyesight began to deteriorate steadily
due to the formation of cataracts – she had worn spectacles for
some years previously – and it failed to respond to treatment
with belladonna. Reading became increasingly difficult; her
Assistant Private Secretary, Sir Frederick Ponsonby, ordered

blacker ink and thicker paper until the Queen complained that it was difficult to fit into the despatch boxes, when he confessed himself finally beaten. Until the very end, though, she retained an amazing grasp of both family and national affairs. She was still 'Grandmamma' to monarchs throughout Europe and she remained their confidante, arbiter and adviser, finding her way with ease and confidence through the intricate labyrinth of family connections. She was everywhere held in affection, awe and veneration. After her death Prince George referred to her as 'one of the greatest women that has ever lived'.

On the outbreak of the Boer War in October, 1899, the Queen, now in her eighty-first year, saw an opportunity she was ever alert for, 'to be of use'. She saw herself as the Head of the Army and she was always careful to wish the departing troops farewell. Refreshed by a new spirit of activity she reviewed the military and visited the wounded. The long years of seclusion were now a thing of the past; she was never again to be thus parted from her people. She ordered 100,000 tins of chocolate to be sent to the men; a few of these containers survive to this day. Above all, she was intensely interested in the progress of the war: she put on an optimistic front when after a few months the tide turned against us: she was 'not interested in the possibilities of defeat'.

In the early months of 1900 the Boers suffered major setbacks: Ladysmith was relieved and, in May, Mafeking was freed from the Boer strangle-hold. The old Queen drove out again jubilantly to share in the wild rejoicing of her subjects. In May she paid a visit to Ireland, a nation deeply divided on the question of Home Rule; she exerted herself to bring about a reconciliation, and by the middle of the year she was tired by all that she had gone through. But the Royal routine continued: the Queen was at Balmoral in the early summer of 1900; then on to Windsor, and down to Osborne again in July. It was there that she was given the news of Affie's death: '*Osborne 31 July, 1900*. A terrible day. When I had hardly finished dressing Lenchen and Beatrice knocked at the door and came in. I at once asked if there were any news, and Lenchen replied, "Yes, bad news, very bad news; he has slept away!" Oh, God! my poor darling Affie gone too! My third grown-up child . . . It is hard at eighty-one! It is so merciful that dearest Affie died in his sleep without any struggle, but it is heart-rending . . .

*Osborne, 1899.* Above: *Queen Victoria with (right) The Prince of Wales (later King Edward VII), (centre) The Duke of York (later King George V) and Prince Edward (later King Edward VIII). In the background, Indian attendant with the Queen's wheelchair.* Below: *The Duchess of York (later Queen Mary) and another lady (centre) – probably Alexandra, Princess of Wales.*

'I was greatly upset, one sorrow, one trial, one anxiety, following another. It is a horrible year, nothing but sadness and horrors of one kind following another . . . Recollections of Affie's childhood and youth, and nowhere more vivid than here, crowded in upon me.

'The whole day was spent in writing and answering telegrams. Lenchen and Beatrice, who feel this sad loss dreadfully, were most helpful. Took a short drive with them after tea round by the sea, and we dined alone together.'[1]

As always she returned to Balmoral for the autumn, where she learned of the death of a grandson, Prince Christian Victor, in South Africa. She was shattered by this accumulation or sorrows and exhausted by increasing insomnia. It was during this last visit to Scotland that 'the first distinct symptoms of a breakdown in her health became apparent. They were of a dyspeptic kind coupled with general nutritional ailments: at Windsor in November signs of slight confusion of speech became evident, indicating that small vessels supplying blood to the brain had become damaged.'[2] Even the weather was against her; the Scottish autumn proved gloomy and depressing and, in the Isle of Wight, unseasonable gales had wrecked the old swimming-bath moored down in the bay.

Back once more at Osborne for Christmas the Queen's condition continued to deteriorate. It is characteristic of her that when the physicians prescribed a lighter diet, substituting Benger's, she often simply added it to the indigestible food she had already demanded. That Christmas Day in 1900 was to be her last, and it was one of her saddest. In the morning she learned of the death in the night of her lifelong friend and companion Jane, Lady Churchill, in another part of the house. As the Queen peered about bemusedly, it was plain that the old order was changing. She went to the Durbar Room to see the Christmas trees but, as she was taken round in her wheel-chair, the candle-light seemed very dim and there was little joy in the time-honoured ceremony. As the New Year of 1901 came round it was becoming clear that the end could not long be delayed, yet to the great majority of the British public Queen Victoria had become a kind of permanent institution. She had reigned longer than any previous English Monarch; few now could remember her accession. She was 'the Grandmother of Europe' and it seemed almost inconceivable that she would die.

# 19

## The Queen's Death at Osborne

*1 January, 1901.* Another year begun, and I am feeling so weak and unwell that I enter upon it sadly. The same sort of night as I have been having lately, but I did get rather more sleep and was up earlier. Lenchen and Beatrice came and wished me a happy New Year, as did also Thora; the others I saw later. Heaps of telegrams, letters, and cards, which Lenchen and Beatrice kindly answered for me. In the afternoon I drove with Arthur and Thora, and we went down to the Soldiers' Home, where there are some convalescents from South Africa. I said a few words to them, thanking them for their services. . . . Then we drove to Whippingham and called on Mr. Clement Smith* who came out to the carriage and spoke to us. Rested when I came home.[1]

By now the Queen no longer attended services in the Chapel at the end of the House: '*Sunday, 6 Jan. 1901.* At five had a short service in the drawing-room like the other day. The ladies and some of the gentlemen and servants were present. We had three hymns, one very pretty one, the Vesper hymn. Only the choir boys sang, and Beatrice accompanied on the harmonium. Mr. Clement Smith officiated. Had my supper of Benger's Food, which is very soothing and nourishing, after which Ismay (Southampton) came and read to me, and then Lenchen and Beatrice sat with me for awhile. Saw Sir Francis Laking, who is here to relieve Sir James Reid a little.'[2]

During the previous week the Queen had received Lord Roberts, the Commander-in-Chief of the British forces in South Africa, who had come to report on the progress of the Boer War and to give her news of the death of Prince Christian Victor. After he had seen the Prince's mother, Princess Christian, he was

* Rector of St. Mildred's, Whippingham.

123

received by the Queen, who spoke to him for half an hour and then conferred on him the Order of the Garter and an Earldom. Having lost her grandson in South Africa, she took a deep and personal interest in the war.

It was clear, however, that the Queen was far from well. She continued to comment on the affairs of the day but her Acting Private Secretary, Sir Frederick Ponsonby, took precautions for withholding unwelcome news from the Queen, fearing to aggravate her condition. A spell of stormy weather prevented her from taking her drives daily but she was out in the carriage with her ladies whenever possible. On 13 January she made the final entry in her Journal, kept almost unbroken for nearly seventy years:

> Had a fair night but was a little wakeful. Got up earlier and had some milk. Lenchen came and read some papers. Out before one, in the garden chair, Lenchen and Beatrice going with me. Rested a little, had some food, and took a short drive with Lenchen and Beatrice. Rested when I came in and at five-thirty went down to the drawing-room, where a short service was held by Mr. Clement Smith, who performed it so well, and it was a great comfort to me. Rested again afterwards, then did some signing, and dictated to Lenchen.[3]

She did not go out again. There had been so many walks, so many drives; what thoughts must have passed through her sleepy mind as, dozing on and off, she ambled along those familiar gravelled walks? Here she had strolled with Albert and beyond, on the slope of the valley, they had built the snowman with Affie's hat on its head, in that cold winter of 1859. Osborne held so many memories.

The next day, the Queen held her last audiences, receiving again Lord Roberts, and Mr. Joseph Chamberlain. On the 15th she sat in her pony-chaise with Marie, Affie's widow, waiting for her drive, but the weather did not clear and she returned indoors.

On the 17th the Queen suffered a slight stroke. The Household sprang into action and the Royal family were summoned by telegram on the 18th. The next day the Queen rallied a little and the Prince of Wales returned to London. The German Emperor, Wilhelm II, whose strongly anti-British attitude was deeply resented in Britain, upset everyone by his decision to come down to Osborne, but a telegram was despatched advising him to remain in London for the time being. By Saturday the 19th the Queen had entered the last stages of her illness: her physicians noted that her heart beat steadily to the end despite exhaustion of the brain and body: apart from occasional lapses, however, her mind remained clear. There was not suffering, only a great weariness.

By now the great House was packed: the ladies and gentlemen in attendance on members of the Royal family had to be housed in the neighbourhood. On the evening of 21 January the Queen took a turn for the worse and her physicians feared she might not survive the night. Only that morning a bulletin had been issued, signed by Sir James Reid, Dr. R. Douglas Powell and Dr. T. Barlow:

'*8.0 a.m.*
The Queen this morning showed signs of diminishing strength, and Her Majesty's condition again assumes a more serious aspect.'

The Bishop of Winchester was summoned and the Prince of Wales, contacted by telephone, was asked to leave London by special train. By this time, however, the Queen had rallied, and with great difficulty the Prince was again contacted and advised to postpone his departure. 'Fritz' Ponsonby recalls sitting up all night in the huge, silent house waiting for any emergency, and contemplating the future without a Queen.[4] He slept late on the following morning, the 22nd, and came down to find that the Prince of Wales and the German Emperor had arrived. Fortunately, the latter behaved well, only saying: 'I should like to see Grandmamma before she dies, but if that is impossible I shall quite understand.'[5]

By lunchtime the Queen was failing and at four o'clock another bulletin was issued: 'The Queen is slowly sinking.' When the Prince of Wales came in to see her she became conscious for a moment and held out her arms to him, whispering; 'Bertie'. He kissed her and his emotions gave way. In another brief spell of consciousness she asked for her little Pomeranian dog, Turi, and it lay on her bed for a while. It seems likely that by this time the Queen had been moved on to a smaller bed set up in her room, on which she could be more easily nursed and supported. During the late afternoon, as the short winter's day was drawing to its close, the Royal family was summoned. The Queen kept rallying and sinking – as the Duke of Argyll put it – like a great three-decker man-of-war. For two and a half hours the German Emperor supported her in his arms, with Sir James Reid on her other side. Around her bed stood the closest members of her immense family. Prayers were said by the Bishop and Mr. Clement Smith, whom the Queen had sent for, lest he should feel hurt. The Princes and Princesses called out their names hoping for a sign of recognition, falling silent as the Queen lapsed into a coma, quietly slipping away. The Bishop of Winchester noted that at about half-past six, 'Came a great change of look and complete calmness'. The owner of Osborne was dead.

The House was ringed with police until the authorities had been officially informed of the Queen's death. At 6.45 the last Bulletin was issued: 'Her Majesty the Queen breathed her last, surrounded by her children and grandchildren.' At the same time the new King telegraphed the Lord Mayor of London: 'My beloved Mother, the Queen, has just passed away, surrounded by her children and grandchildren. Albert Edward.' When the news was released to the crowd at the gates, the pall of silence which had covered the immediate area was shattered. A horde of yelling journalists cycled madly down the long hill into Cowes to telephone, 'Queen dead!' which was swiftly telegraphed around the world. It was the end of an era. A sense of profound loss was experienced throughout Europe: all that the Queen had stood for – prosperity, power, stability – seemed with her passing to have vanished. Princess May summed it up in her diary: 'At about 10 we had a short service in her bedroom, darling Grandmamma looked so lovely and peaceful all in white with lace, and the bed covered with flowers. The thought of England without the Queen is dreadful even to think of. God help us all.'[6]

## 20

## Queen Victoria's Departure from Osborne

The Queen left in her will minute instructions regarding her funeral. Black was forbidden; purple and white were to be ordered; the key note was to be one of brightness and light, and so it was. A master of all ceremonial, the Queen excelled at funerals. While her body still lay in her bedroom it was viewed by members of the Household and servants. Undertakers were excluded and when the coffin, made from timber cut on the Osborne estate, was delivered, she was lifted into it by the Prince of Wales and the Duke of Connaught: they were surprised that she had become so light. On the Wednesday three hundred tenants filed through the Dining-Room, whither it had by then been borne, to see the coffin on a small dais. On 27 January Princess May, the future Queen Mary, wrote: 'The Queen looked so beautiful after death, like a marble statue and much younger. Now she lies in her coffin in the Dining-Room which is beautifully arranged as a chapel, the coffin is covered with the coronation robes and her little diamond crown and the garter lie on a cushion above her head – 4 huge Grenadiers watch there day and night, it is so impressive and fine, yet so simple. You would howl if you could see it all – We go from time to time and the feeling of peace in that room is most soothing to one's feelings.'[1]

On Friday, 1 February, the Queen's last journey from Osborne began. During the morning masses of people from all over the Island, as well as from the mainland, converged upon Osborne to line York Avenue down the hill to East Cowes. Within the grounds tenants and invited officials took up their positions: two Royal Marine bands arrived, and just before one o'clock the gun carriage of the Royal Horse Artillery drew up at the Queen's entrance. There was an extraordinary stillness: for some minutes it seemed as though the House were uninhabited, but a last short service was being held in the Dining-Room for the family. The Queen's Company of the Grenadier Guards was drawn up in the forecourt and at half-past one on that still, clear winter's afternoon bluejackets from the Royal Yacht carried the Queen's coffin down the steps, placing it on the gun-carriage, where it was covered by a pall. The crown and garter were replaced, and the orb and sceptre of the coronation regalia, symbols of her sixty-four years' rule, lay at the foot. To the sparkle of helmets and the nodding of plumes, and to the strains of the Black Watch funeral dirge, the cortège moved off with the Mourners led by the new King, the German Emperor and the Duke of Connaught following behind the gun-carriage. In sharp contrast to the pall of cream satin worked with the Royal Arms was the deep mourning and heavy veiling of the Royal ladies in the procession. The pipers played 'The Flowers of the Forest' and, as the cortège passed through the Queen's Entrance into York Avenue, the bands with their muffled drums broke into Beethoven's Funeral March.

At Trinity Pier the *Alberta* lay waiting. The quarter-deck had been covered with an awning from which curtains had been hung at each corner. The deck was carpeted and in the middle stood the catafalque draped with a crimson cloth lined with white silk. On this brilliant February afternoon the Medina River was crowded with craft with their flags at half-mast and beyond, stretching away out of sight beyond the point, the warships of the Channel Fleet formed two parallel lines down Spithead. By half-past two, when the cortège drew up, the tide was low, and the bluejackets carrying the Queen's coffin on board the *Alberta* had a steeply-inclined gangway to negotiate. At three o'clock all was arranged and the ship drew away from the quay with the yachts *Victoria and Albert, Osborne* and *Hohenzollern* and *Enchantress* taking up position in line astern. As the little vessel passed between the ships of the fleet the minute guns thundered out and smoke drifted across a sky that was red and gold. The mourners and members of the Household following in their yachts saw, receding from view, the pavilion on the beach where the Queen had sat watching her children and grandchildren playing and, beyond the bare trees, the balcony under its green and white canopy, where she and her beloved husband had stood hand in hand listening to the nightingales.

*Part Two*

Since 1901

## 21

## Royal Naval College, Osborne

The months following Queen Victoria's death were a dark period in the history of Osborne. The Household dwindled, furniture was draped with holland covers and the rooms were locked. A sepulchral silence settled on the Pavilion Wing. King Edward VII had spent much time and money on his estate at Sandringham, which he certainly did not wish to relinquish, and he had little use therefore for Osborne, which cannot have held many happy memories for him. His craving for society would in any case have precluded Osborne, across the water on the Island, from being an easily accessible private residence. At the same time, the King wished to stand by the terms of his mother's will, which expressed the hope that Osborne would remain in the family who would each retain a share in the property.

No one wanted it. In December, 1901, King Edward, firmly backed by Queen Alexandra, offered it to Prince George and Princess May. They turned it down. The Princess wrote: 'Just returned from tea with Motherdear. She spoke to me about Osborne . . . she says that of course if we cannot take it the old place will have to go to rack and ruin. I told her we were going to talk it over & see what could be done.'[1] The fact remained that they did not want it: Osborne had become a white elephant. The great house was shut and the army of retainers shrank, some going into retirement, while others had been absorbed into the new Royal Household. Sheeted and deserted, but still filled with the bric-à-brac dear to an old lady's heart, the House awaited the King's decision.

In the face of a strong resistance from each of his family to the King's wish to grant Osborne to them as a residence, Edward VII finally capitulated. On his Coronation Day he wrote from Buckingham Palace to the Prime Minister, Mr. Balfour: '. . . The King feels that he is unable to make adequate use of Osborne as a

Royal Residence, and accordingly he has determined to offer the
property in the Isle of Wight as a gift to the Nation . . .'[2]

It was from the first the King's intention that Osborne should
be used as a Convalescent Home for Officers of the Army and
Navy. Like most plans, this one evolved only gradually. It was
originally intended that officers should occupy bed-sitting-rooms
each with its telephone. Special furniture was manufactured and
unusually high beds were introduced to facilitate nursing. Preparations were made to open the State rooms to the public but, by
the King's wish, the private apartments were closed by bronzed
gates, through which only the House Governor and the cleaners
might pass. The Queen's bedroom became a kind of family
shrine and, especially during Cowes Week, members of the Royal
Family quietly came to Osborne to meditate in the room where
'Grandmama' died. Meanwhile the conversion of the Main and
Household Wings proceeded steadily.

The plan to make use of Osborne as a Royal Naval College
originated in the fertile minds of Lord Esher and Admiral Sir
John Fisher, who, during his appointment as Commander-in-
Chief in the Mediterranean, began his assessment of the state of
the nation's armed forces which was to culminate in a complete
reorganisation of the Navy. It was due to the foresight of this
brilliant and forceful officer that Britain was ready to meet the
challenge of Germany in 1914. By the end of the nineteenth century, the old wooden training ship H.M.S. *Britannia* which, together with her sister ship H.M.S. *Hindustan*, formed the
Royal Naval College, Dartmouth, had come to the end of her
useful life. The building of a new College ashore was already
under way but it would not be ready until 1905. Fisher argued that
a modern Navy in which full use of the most up-to-date technology was to be made was of prime importance to a nation to
which supremacy at sea was vital. In conjunction with Lord Sel-
borne, Fisher took the first steps towards the fulfilment of their
plan to re-create the 'grass roots' of the Navy. A site had first to
be found; as a result, perhaps, of his good relationship with King
Edward VII Fisher suggested that the grounds of Osborne House
might be made available. The King readily agreed and work soon
commenced.

An area was found to the south of the house bordering the
edge of the original estate which would suit admirably. The
coach-house was to be converted to a central block, to be called

'St. Vincent', with offices, hall, and chapel; and the stables which would become the classrooms. The cadets were to be housed in dormitories like long, low bungalows with plunge-bath and wash-rooms at the ends. Opposite, on the other side of a connecting corridor, each dormitory had its own reading-room, which was used for quiet occupations and private study. A mast complete with yards, shrouds and rigging was erected in front of 'Nelson' Block and its base was surrounded by a safety net. On one occasion when cadets were 'Manning the yards' a boy fell. On landing his head broke through the net but he was saved by his shoulders. During the history of the College there was no serious accident recorded by falling from the mast. Games fields were laid out in the park between Osborne House and Barton Manor and the buildings, which were prefabricated in sections clad with a material called Uralite, went up quickly. There was provision for boat work on the Medina River at Cowes and on the east bank an engineering workshop was built. It was a part of the Fisher-Selborne Plan that there should be a strong engineering bias in the training and that cadets destined for that Branch of the Service should enter in the same way as General List – or Seaman – Cadets. Indeed, preference was to be shown to those Cadets who would accept entry into the Engineering Branch.

On 14 August 1903 the College was nearly ready, at least to accept the first entry of Cadets aged between 12 years 8 months and 13 years. They would spend two years of three terms each at Osborne, two years more at Dartmouth and a further three years training at sea as Midshipmen. On this day King Edward, who had been yachting during Cowes Week, formally opened the new College, in which he was to display a continuing interest during his reign. The King must have been aware of a certain irony in letting loose into those hallowed grounds a swarm of noisy young boys, but he was modern in outlook and practical in his attitude towards Osborne.

The opening was reported in *The Illustrated London News:* 'The College in the Isle of Wight is utilitarian to the last degree; so much so as to render any criticism of the buildings from an artistic point of view quite out of the question . . . The stables at Osborne House formed the nucleus of the new building; and in close proximity to these, which were promptly adapted for various purposes – there were run up a series of bungalow erections – dormitories, officers' quarters, and so on – constructed of timber . . . They are very well fitted and up to date. There are twenty-five beds in a dormitory; each cadet's chest stands at the foot of his bed, and a wash-basin beside it; there is a plunge-bath, with three ordinary ones, at the end of the dormitory, and a capital lavatory system, for use in the day-time.'[3]

The first cadets arrived on 15 September, a party of 80 small boys, proudly resplendent in their new uniforms, on the very threshold of their Naval careers. In more than one sense they had already come a long way. The recruiting grounds for the Wardrooms of the navy were the preparatory schools which had grown rapidly in number to supply the educational needs of the Victorian middle class. Their philosophy was simple and wholesome – a healthy mind in a healthy body – and they closely followed the precepts of Arnold of Rugby and Thring of Uppingham. Their curriculum broadened out from Classics and Christianity to include Mathematics and Science, and games assumed a new significance. Fees at Osborne were fixed at £25 per term and parents were responsible for supplying the uniforms and all their sons' requirements. Entrance was by selection board which assessed with some degree of success a boy's probable response to naval discipline and the general demands of a career at sea; a stringent 'medical' including a stiff eyesight test was followed by academic examinations in London which lasted four or five days. It followed then that the Navy had the pick of the eager youth of the country – but only from the middle and upper classes of society. There was then no machinery in existence by which a talented boy from the working classes could join the Navy as an officer, though he might after proven good service be promoted Warrant Officer. There is no doubt that they were immensely proud; they were joining what was then the largest and finest fighting service in the world with a tradition that reached back through the centuries. For many of them that tradition was embedded deep in their families; fathers and uncles were already at sea. The Royal family had strong links with the sea: King William IV, Queen Victoria's uncle, had been a sailor; her son, Prince Alfred entered the Navy as a Midshipman, and her grandson, Prince George, by then Prince of Wales, was a keen and professional seaman who in his own right achieved the rank of Captain.

For this generation of cadets life was apparently secure and privileged but even then the eyes of the nation's leaders were turned doubtfully towards Germany. At all events, the lucky ones, perhaps a half to two-thirds of those who attended the Selection Board, were accepted. Often, the first news a boy received of his success was a communication from Mr. Gieve, a Naval outfitter, who desired attendance for the measuring of the new uniform. At the beginning of every new term a Gieve's representative was always present at Portsmouth before the Cadets embarked for the trip to Cowes. Whether or not a Cadet was on the firm's books, the representative performed the useful service of smoothing out many initial difficulties.

Awaiting this first 'term' of Cadets at Osborne were Captain R. E. Wemyss, R.N. with fourteen officers and additional petty officers as their instructors. There were also Mr. Cyril Ashford, the Headmaster, lately senior Science master at Harrow and a team of nine academic staff. From the first, it was apparent that the College was very well run and, although the life was rigorous, the routine strict and the academic curriculum exacting, there is no reason to believe that the Cadets were unhappy. Quite clearly, from the evidence in the *Osborne Magazine*, an immense amount of careful planning went into the Cadets' programme.

On arrival at the College the new term, which was called after a famous admiral, was accommodated in two or three of the dormitories. The term was divided into Port and Starboard Watches, according to their position on the examination pass list. Already their Naval training had begun. The Naval ceremonies of 'Colours' and 'Sunset' morning and evening were meticulously observed to raise and lower the White Ensign at the mast. They moved at the double, learned to salute and attended lessons in uniform. On the other hand, these self-same lessons were conducted by civilians, who had somehow infiltrated into the Service; games were run on school lines and there was a well-patronised tuck-shop, where Cadets bought fruit and paper-bags of sweets called 'Mouldies'.

There was a prevailing tendency natural enough among cadets in such a Naval situation to regard the civilian staff as 'second class citizens'. Lord Mountbatten recalls that he was caught sucking a 'Mouldie' in class by one 'Mossybags' Warner, and was given a chit awarding him two extra drills as a punishment: 'I despised him for it,' he added. Masters seemed to have little real power of their own. If they happened to own or sail a boat it brought them nearer to the Naval instructors, but in the cadets' eyes they were privileged in being permitted to partake of Service life.

The day began early with the Cadets rising at 6.30 a.m., when they stripped off their pyjamas and ran down the dormitory and through the plunge-bath before dressing. In especially cold weather, with the keen wind from the Solent piercing the prefabricated walls, it must have been a chilly experience but the dormitories and reading rooms were heated by primitive, solid-fuel stoves, and a sense of urgency in the boys' routine assisted their circulation. After breakfast cadets paraded for 'Colours' and went to their classrooms. There was a 'break' for milk and soda and buns or Garibaldi biscuits, after which instruction continued until lunch. In the afternoons, and sometimes in the mornings, watches were marched in 'Fours' under a petty officer and a Cadet Captain chosen from a senior term, to the workshops at Kingston. There they learned the rudiments of metalwork and engineering drawing and studied some of the machinery to be found on board ship. Rugger and some soccer, with cricket in the summer, formed the basis of the sporting programme. In the summer especially there were other activities; athletics, boatwork and swimming. Cadets bathed at first down in Osborne Bay but this was later forbidden and parties were taken to nearby beaches. There was no swimming bath. A cadet captain of 1904 recalls that he passed his swimming test before he could use the 'blue boats' on the Medina in the dormitory plunge where he went round and round like a goldfish in a bowl under the eye of an officer.

Once a term there was a whole holiday: the teams went off to an 'away' match with other schools and many Cadets were taken in horse-drawn vehicles to picnic places on the Island. There was a holiday atmosphere, the boys wearing shorts and white cotton sun hats which emphasised their youthfulness. There were games when Cadets under the supervision of masters went up on to Brightstone Down, or swam when they were taken to Colwell or Totland Bays. It was a day in which they could relax if they found the Naval climate of Osborne perhaps too bracing; the conversation was nautical larded with prep school expressions. This was part of the unique flavour of Osborne. The Cadets were clearly no longer 'prep school boys' they were officers in embryo;

they were old enough to join the lowest echelons of public schools but there was seldom a Cadet in the College over the age of fifteen. Osborne, then, offered them a staging post in their transition to manhood, and their boyish enthusiasms were carefully cultivated while the weaknesses of childhood gradually fell away.

There was little or no bullying at Osborne. The old Royal Naval College at Dartmouth consisted of two hulks, the *Britannia* and the *Hindustan* which were connected to one another by a covered gangway. In the earliest days life was as tough as Tom Brown's Rugby: there was a tradition of fagging, the 'News' or first termers fetching and carrying for the seniors, or 'Sixers'. It was even recorded that sweating teams of 'News' would be made to carry 'Sixers' bodily up the hill to the tuck shop and games fields. The food had been bad and discipline entrusted to ship's corporals who misunderstood or mishandled their duties. The new College, now building, would ensure that the worst evils were not perpetuated. At Osborne, though, intense rivalry between terms quickly manifested itself, but it was a healthy competitive spirit which showed itself in games and in an elaborate affair called 'Assault at Arms' which was held regularly. There was fencing and boxing, a tug-o'-war team and boat pulling in pair-oars on the river.

Relationships with both officers and masters was good; Cadets were taken out sailing and invited to tea at the officers' homes. There was a genuine interest in the Cadets as individuals and as future mess-mates; in a sense, even their outings and the contact with grown-ups was part of their training. The river gave the Cadets a new dimension in their lives, for most of them it was a new skill to be acquired and it gave them a sense of responsibility through the difficulty they experienced in controlling the boats on the fast tidal streams. The Regattas were major events and greatly looked forward to; not only did the Cadets take part, they enjoyed the pulling races between the officers and the teaching staff; the landing stages at Kingston were lined with young figures in white duck.

Meals at Osborne were formal. In keeping with the times the Cadets were waited upon by Cadet-Stewards, often Naval pensioners, who also looked after their laundry and dormitories. The food was, during the early years at least, very good, though the quality understandably deteriorated during the war, when it became difficult to maintain the high standard. An apocryphal story relates that King Edward VII visiting the College in its early days insisted that the Cadets should be well fed, and ordered a member of his own catering staff to take charge of affairs under the Paymaster. 'Palmer,' he said, 'see to it that the Cadets are properly fed – good food, too.' At all events, at that time they fed like fighting cocks, with chicken, then more of a luxury than it is today, on Sundays.

The glamour conferred by being part of the Navy never palled. There was something rather special about going to a rugger match against a preparatory school in one of the College steam pinnaces. On the College's own terms the Cadets could go far afield, and were encouraged to do so. An admiral's widow on the other side of the Solent often invited parties of boys to tea, and a whole term also had tea with Admiral and Lady Fisher at Admiralty House in the Dockyard at Portsmouth. Only in the company of parents, however, might a Cadet walk down to visit Cowes.

There were days, too, when the College was *en fête*; due both to its novelty and to its proximity to London, illustrious visitors were a commonplace at Osborne. The Cadets quickly became used to the interruptions to the routine and even grew to resent them. During the summer term parents were invited and there is an air of gaiety in the old photographs which would be hard to recapture today. The morning coats and top hats of the gentlemen, no less than the long skirts, feathers and elaborate millinery of the ladies confer an immediate impression of pre-war wealth and ease. The Cadets, immaculate in their uniforms, with the buttons rather high upon the chest and the caps rather small in the crown, are everywhere to be seen amongst the crowd. The sense of purpose behind the Fisher-Selborne plan could not have been divined in that social scene.

Those ten years before the outbreak of war were the best in the history of Osborne. If the spirit of the old Queen and her Court lay behind the darkened, shuttered Pavilion wing, at which Cadets returning from their swim at the beach so often glanced, the College itself hummed with a new, young life. It prospered steadily under the critical but benevolent eye of 'Jackie' Fisher who came often from Portsmouth, and of the King himself who on occasion addressed the Cadets in his guttural accents. There was a feeling of security that smacked of arrogance and was symbolised by the unashamed gentility which prevailed and was manifested in those swaying watch-chains and parasols which were so marked a feature of Parents' Days. Tragedy still lay below the horizon. In those first years, stability and determination to maintain the superiority of the Navy were the prevailing themes.

In 1907 King Edward's grandson, Prince Edward, arrived at Osborne as a Cadet. This young boy of twelve was later to become King Edward VIII and, after his abdication in 1936, the Duke of Windsor. In his own account of his life at Osborne he recorded that he was bewildered by the transition from a world of tutors and (comparative) segregation from boys of his own age to the noisy bustle of Osborne. As the son of the Prince of W(h)ales, he was, of course, known as 'Sardine'. Upon the whole the Prince was well received. True, on one occasion a sash window was lowered on to his neck to remind him of the fate of one of his wayward ancestors, Charles I, and on another a bottle of red ink was poured down his neck, which resulted in his missing parade and being awarded extra drills.[4] He was quiet and un-assuming and he found ready acceptance amongst the Cadets.

In due course Edward was joined by his brother Prince Albert, 'Bertie', whose physical frailty was not altogether suited to the Osborne conditions, and later still, Prince George, Duke of Kent, passed through the College and served with the Royal Navy until 1929. There followed Prince George of Battenberg and his brother, Prince Louis, later the Earl Mountbatten of Burma. The Princes led a refreshingly normal life, being treated in the same way as the other Cadets. On Sundays there was 'Divisions', a formal parade and Church Service, after which Cadets might go out for the day with relatives. The Princes were often enter-tained by Princess Beatrice who lived just down the road at Osborne Cottage. Perhaps she may have felt her brother's decision to close Osborne House was, in the end, justified by all that she saw and heard of the College.

The Princes were clearly able to adjust to their surroundings; they quickly learned the College traditions, however new those might be. The Duke of Windsor recorded that he could not be seen in conversation with a Cadet younger than himself, and therefore arranged to meet his younger brother at the far side of the sports field. The Prince quailed at the thought of his termly reports; after two rather discouraging terms the third showed

improvement. The Prince was so overcome that when he was summoned to his father's study, he burst into tears, and we are instantly reminded of the identical reaction of Prince Albert Edward, Queen Victoria's son, some forty-five years earlier, when his awe-inspiring parents sent him a memorandum signed by them both on the subject of the Duty of a Royal Prince.

The letters of young Prince Louis of Battenberg reflect a complete and unreserved acceptance of his Cadetship. His father, Admiral Prince Louis of Battenberg, who was married to a grand-daughter of Queen Victoria, had been appointed First Sea Lord, and his son, 'Dickie' as he was known by friends and family alike, entered the Service enthusiastically. He wrote regularly and frankly to his parents and the letters to his mother show a proper concern for the necessities of Osborne life. His financial affairs are complex and birthday presents assume real importance as the time drew near. Lapses in handwriting are accounted for by 'writing in bed', or by 'a fierce dormitory raid' which was impeding his efforts. On the other hand, his accounts of Osborne affairs are dealt with in detail and with considerable relish:

On Friday night I heard the best lecture I have or, probably, ever will hear, in my life. It lasted from 8 until 10 p.m. All the officers, masters, bluejackets, marines, instructors, stewards, some bluejackets from Portsmouth; the families of all these people and many more of the staff were listening to it, so there must have been eight hundred to a thousand in the room. It was given by Commander Evans on the Scott Expedition. There were hundreds of lantern slides, and a whole cinematograph film. The clapping, yelling, stamping, cheering was such that I've still got a sore throat from it . . . He then gave us his theodolite. The way he gave his lecture and spoke about the two seamen who saved his life was marvellous . . .[5]

The note of youthful hero-worship is unmistakable.

Another event that took place early in the careers of the cadets during the first generations to pass through Osborne was the week's cruise in H.M.S. *Racer*. This was an old gunboat which

*Royal Naval College, Osborne, January 1909. Prince Edward (later King Edward VIII) seated third from left, Prince Albert (later King George VI) on ground, centre*

served as a tender to the College. Each term of Cadets, under the
supervision of a depleted permanent crew, took her for a gentle
cruise in local waters. It imparted a sense of real achievement
and, by the time the ship returned to her moorings in Cowes
Roads, every Cadet had taken a turn in each department. The
social round, too, emphasised the pleasures and opportunities of
going ashore, pleasures which have been part and parcel of the
seafaring tradition since time immemorial. In this account, from
a Cadet's Journal of 1905, his transformation into a Naval
Officer even in his first term, can be discerned:

We embarked on Sunday evening and on Monday morning
steamed down to the Needles and anchored at the entrance to
the Hamble River. On Tuesday we went ashore to have tea
with Lady Fullerton and a game of footer. On Wednesday we
returned to the buoy in Cowes Roads and went up to the College for the Trafalgar Night sing-song. We got back at 11.0
p.m. Thursday: at noon we arrived at Portsmouth and after
going round the Dockyard and visiting the sail and rigging
lofts and H.M.S. *Caesar*, we went to tea with Sir John and
Lady Fisher and had the honour of being the only class who
cleared the tea-table to the last crumb. Next day, Friday, the
*Neptune*, an old battleship, sold out of the Navy to a German
firm, was to have left in tow of a powerful tug. The tide caught
her ... and she bore down on the *Racer* – when within 20
yards the towing hawser parted, and she drifted up the harbour with the tide, and in a few minutes struck the *Victory* at
the port gangway. Next day we returned to Cowes.[6]

The description of the *Neptune*'s mishap is clearly described
in the technical language of the Navy and with an eye for
detail. There is still the small boy, with his vast appetite and his
'footer', but a professional interest is already evident in movements, places and events.

The College grew apace. Each term some 80 Cadets arrived
and after two years there were over four hundred Cadets under
training.

There seemed to be a single flaw in the system: the health
record of Osborne might not withstand careful investigation.
The causes were obscure. Conjunctivitis, or 'pink-eye' was
more or less endemic; the Cadets put it down to the fact that

the classrooms had been converted from the old stables. But there were other, and more serious, complications. On reading term by term the obituary notices of Cadets who died, either at Park House, where Cadets were sent from the Sick Bay, or at home, or in hospital, we are forcibly struck by their comparatively large number. The first death occurred, apparently from pneumonia, in 1907, to be followed by a small but steady stream. During the Easter Term, 1917, six boys died during an epidemic of measles – but then measles in those days before the development of antibiotics could be a killer. It may be conjectured that some boys found the transition from the warmth and comforts of home life to the rigours of Osborne too much for their constitutions: either they were withdrawn or they simply grew out of it. Young Prince Louis of Battenberg lost a great deal of time in his first year languishing in the Sick Bay or at Park House; a temperature and sore throat seemed to persist for an unduly long time. For all that it offered the Osborne life was no bed of roses, yet this too was perhaps in the best traditions of the Service.

In 1909 the College emerged into a sudden and unwelcome prominence. A Cadet by the name of Archer-Shee had been found guilty by the Captain-Superintendent of stealing a five-shilling postal order from the locker of one of his mess-mates. The boy pleaded his innocence but his parents were asked to withdraw their son from the Navy. An appeal by the parents to Captain Christian was refused and further appeals to the Board of Admiralty to reconsider the findings were made in vain. Eventually, the Admiralty allowed an endorsement of the Petition of Right and the case was taken to Court.[7] The Cadet was vindicated and his innocence was publicly declared amid scenes of wild excitement. The family was broken financially by the protracted legal battle and Archer-Shee did not return to the Navy; but the wording of the Endorsement 'Let Right be Done', under the signature of King Edward VII, was seen to be upheld. The case was the subject of a successful play, *The Winslow Boy* by Terence Rattigan. In 1914 the ex-Cadet was commissioned in the army and was killed at Ypres a month after the outbreak of war.

Naval discipline could be severe. The Duke of Windsor recalls the caning of a Cadet, the son of the Captain at the time, E. S. Alexander-Sinclair, for numerous misdemeanours. In front of all the Cadets the boy was strapped down on a vaulting horse and

the caning administered with full Naval ceremony. As a deter-
rent it no doubt had its effect, but it might have proved something
of a shock to a nervous boy who, like Prince Edward, stood in
awe of his father. This kind of punishment, it must be emphasised, was exceptional: Prince Louis relates a similar event in
1914, but most offences were dealt with by the award of a number of extra drills. Following Naval custom offending Cadets
were placed in the Commander's report and appeared before him
in the morning. More serious matters were referred after a preliminary investigation to the Captain. The power of senior
Cadets, the Cadet-Captains, was strictly limited but their influence was considerable. They wore a distinctive ring of gold lace
on one or both arms and were responsible in particular for regu-
lating discipline in the dormitories. A despot could make life un-
pleasant for his dormitory for there could in such circumstances
be no recourse to a higher authority.

Money, borrowing and lending of tuck, and the pursuit of
hobbies were all of great importance in a Cadet's life. They were
given a shilling pocket money weekly, to which they could add
two shillings from their own accounts. Thus they could spend an
average of sixpence a day on almost every day of the week. It
went a long way at the College tuck-shop, and there was nowhere
else to spend it. Fines were imposed for breakages; a broken
window cost threepence and was stopped from the shilling allow-
ance. Parcels of 'tuck' could be sent from home and Sunday
outings afforded opportunities for re-stocking one's private
store. For the many Cadets who stayed 'on board' after Sunday
Divisions there was little to do. The day was less organised and
there was a relative freedom to enjoy – within the College bounds
– a walk with friends down to Osborne Bay or to take part in informal games and activities.

In 1912 His Majesty's Inspectors of Schools arrived at the College. For three days in May they investigated the academic curriculum; the Naval aspect and matters of discipline, being under
the Naval Discipline Act, were outside their terms of reference.
Their report was favourable. They found the time-table somewhat arduous but not unduly so; it occupied $38\frac{3}{4}$ hours a week,
including 'prep' and Religious Instruction and, as we have seen,
a significant proportion set aside for Engineering. The teaching,
they agreed, was imaginative and of a high standard and, in
short, they felt that the education at Osborne was reasonably

comprehensive and sound. It would be interesting to know what these very experienced Inspectors really felt about the whole spectrum of College life, but this was something which could not be recorded.

In 1914, early in the summer holidays, the Great War broke out. The Fleet had already mobilised and there was a sudden and unprecedented demand for young officers; at one time five hundred cadets a year were entering Osborne, all with, as Lord Mountbatten comments, 'the prospect of becoming Admirals.' Drastic measures were called for to ensure adequate manning of ships. The entire complement of Dartmouth Cadets were sent to sea, even if they had only just arrived. Tragedy struck swiftly: through sheer ineptitude three cruisers, coincidentally under the orders of Admiral Christian, of the Archer-Shee case, were torpedoed by the same U-Boat, two of them while motionless in the water picking up survivors from the third. Among hundreds of officers and men twelve Cadets lost their lives, all of them under the age of fifteen. The Admiralty revised its plans; it was felt that this was too young for Cadets to experience war conditions at sea, but already the *Osborne Magazine* was printing its first Roll of Honour.

The war brought other changes: Captain Rudolph Bentinck, R.N., and a number of his Naval Staff were appointed to more active posts and were replaced by distinctly elderly officers some of whom emerged from retirement to spend the war years at Osborne; the period of training at Osborne was cut from six to five terms and the fortunes – decidedly indifferent at first – of the Navy at sea were followed with lively interest. The *Magazine* ran eye-witness accounts by former Cadets of Naval actions, and it was felt that the War had come to Osborne. Nearby, the Convalescent Home of the House was accepting wounded officers for recuperation. The Solent and Spithead were no longer full of yachts on a summer's day but the smoke from warships rose along the horizon.

In October a devastating blow fell upon one Cadet. Prince Louis of Battenberg, the First Sea Lord, was accused in the Press of having pro-German sympathies to the extent that the early misfortunes of the Navy were ascribed to him. Gallantly, Prince Louis offered his resignation, in the interests of the country, to Mr. Winston Churchill, then First Lord of the Admiralty, who accepted it with the greatest reluctance. Prince Louis quietly retired, an all but broken man, from the supreme eminence to which a Naval officer can aspire.

Some of the opprobrium fell upon his son, 'Dickie', then in his second year as an Osborne Cadet. He silently endured a period of desperate isolation due, in part, to some ill-natured taunts from mess-mates but, also, to the inarticulate sympathy which school-boys show by leaving the sufferer to himself. His unhappy position was ameliorated after a time by the deep resentment voiced by the Fleet at his father's resignation, for Prince Louis had been an outstandingly able and popular Admiral. It seems likely that this event proved a turning-point in the life of young Prince Louis. The fourteen year old boy hero-worshipped his father and had passed easily enough on his own merits into Osborne, one of a large class of 82 Cadets in the Exmouth Term of May, 1913. He was lively and enterprising, as his letters home reveal, and possessed a large capacity for enjoyment which, while in no way quenched, was sublimated by the awful events of 1914 into a fierce and undeviating ambition to vindicate his father. That he succeeded so completely is not a matter for conjecture; it is a matter of fact. The fourteen year old Osborne Cadet who cried himself to sleep in anger and humiliation carved his family name deep on the pages of the history of the Second World War and its aftermath; First Sea Lord, Supreme Allied Commander South East Asia, last Viceroy of India and Chief of the Defence Staff.

*

With the ending of hostilities on 11 November, 1918, the Royal Naval College showed every sign of becoming redundant. Almost every Naval officer under the age of thirty had passed through the College, which was showing evidence of heavy wear and tear. As early as 1907 the Uralite outer panels of the building could have holes kicked in them without even hurting the foot. The elderly instructors withdrew once more into retirement and a new generation of Naval staff appeared who had taken an active part in the war at sea. What was much more to the point was that the Navy had by now become over-manned. As war-worn

*Osborne House today. The site of the Royal Naval College was behind the house. In the background, the River Medina*

ships were put into Reserve categories and not replaced there was insufficient employment for officers. The situation became so acute that redundancies became inevitable. The 'Geddes Axe' fell and officers were compulsorily retired.

It was found that Dartmouth would be fully able to supply the dwindling needs of the Service and plans were made to close Osborne. By the end of 1920 there were barely sixty cadets where four years earlier there had been five hundred, and it was increasingly difficult to sustain morale. During the previous October Torpedo Boat No. 116 was preparing to transfer to Dartmouth – the week long cruises in *Racer* had long been discontinued as being detrimental to the Cadets' general studies – and an old steam launch, formerly the *Beta* but renamed H.M.S. *Osborne*, was also transferred as being surplus to requirements. Some of the instructors and teaching staff were to move down to Dartmouth with the last term of Cadets.

The closing of any large establishment cannot easily be accomplished without some hardship to individuals. The buildings were to be left in charge of four caretakers until the sale of equipment had been completed; one was to live at the workshops down at Kingston. There were a few hitches in the final stages: the last Commanding Officer, Captain C. Royads, R.N. gave way to a Commander Cowan and, finally, only Paymaster Captain C. M. Luckham was left in charge for three weeks after the formal paying off of the College on 20 May, 1921. A request that a Chief Cadet Steward should be allowed to remain as caretaker was apparently ignored: he had been one of the few who had served the College from the time of its inception in 1903: we can only presume that he was pensioned off.

At all events, by the end of that spring in 1921 the halls, dormitories and study rooms, the Wardroom and Petty Officers' Messes were shut, and the playing fields which had been so carefully trimmed and laid out returned to grassland. A silence returned to Osborne which had not been known since the old Queen's death just twenty years previously.

Some dissatisfaction remained: the civilian academic staff of Osborne, who in a sense occupied a unique position in their close relationship with the Royal Navy were compelled to retire, and they were distressed by the small amount of Deferred Pay which they would receive on leaving Osborne. One master, a Mr. Livesey, obliged to retire at the age of fifty-five learned that he would be able to purchase an annuity of only £135, a small reward for long and devoted service. In the aftermath of the war it would be difficult for an elderly master to find another post. The Admiralty received a petition signed by forty past and present members of the academic staff but beyond a further investigation, there could be no redress of grievances.

The College has passed into history and many of those who went there now lie at the bottom of every ocean of the world, often in the tombs of their ships. But still there are those who remember the spacious days of boyhood and meet and share their memories of Osborne, before 'they went down to the sea in ships and carried out their business in great waters'.

Little now remains of that period: the coach-house which was 'St. Vincent' block is now part of the offices of the British Hovercraft Corporation, and two low brick buildings remain, one of which in the grounds of Osborne House has been converted for use by convalescent officers as an occupational therapy centre. The Uralite buildings were quickly demolished and peripheral properties sold off. Today a tarmac car park covers much of the area that was the College and the feet of thousands of visitors tramp where Cadets slept and played and illicitly raced on rollerskates down the long corridor between the dormitories.

## King Edward VII Convalescent Home

Notwithstanding the quarter of a million or so visitors to
Osborne during the summer the primary function of the House
today is as a Convalescent Home. It is open to Officers of the Services and to the Civil Service. At any one time there will be some
forty men and women, young and old, in residence in the Main
and Household wings. The Home is administered by a Council
and is under the direct supervision of a House Governor who is a
retired Medical Officer from one of the Services, whose office is
in the small Audience Room, where in former times Mr. Gladstone tendered his resignation to the Queen – 'I am old and
weary, Ma'am, and in need of rest' – and the Kaiser's son
waited to receive the Garter.

Convalescents usually come to Osborne following illness or
surgery, and the skilled treatment there is adapted to the patients'
needs, varying simply from rest to remedial exercises – a thermal
pool has been installed – and rehabilitation. The atmosphere is
leisurely yet purposeful; during the morning patients undergo
treatment and a number then go across to the Occupational
Therapy department, one of the very few remaining buildings
from the Royal Naval College, where a wide range of activities is
available. Officers who never knew they had it in them, draw,
paint and weave with often surprising results – in every sense.
For the more active the Household Billiard-Room is open, with
croquet on Mount Lawn under the windows of the Prince Consort's Room. Osborne has its own golf course and club-house and
it is ideal for walking, there being a wide area of level ground
near the House. From the Bay residents may sail dinghies and
there is a guest house on the edge of the estate where their
families may stay.

Residents normally arrive on three days of the week and to
help them become acquainted there is a games tournament in

which even the most handicapped can take part: Scrabble, Shove Ha'penny and Draughts indicate the levels of skills and activities. The Council Room with its richly decorated ceiling by Grüner has become the smoking room; near the french windows in the centre stands a large telescope which commands a fine view of the Solent and Spithead. The ladies have their own sitting-room in the Duchess of Kent's suite; the brackets for the canopy over her bed are visible on the wall. The dining-room is the one used by the Household, looking over the south lawn and the great cedar under which Queen Victoria would gather her family for tea and photographs. In the distance, let into the wall of the kitchen garden, is the entrance to the original Osborne House of Lady Blachford; it held sentimental memories for the Queen of their first home.

The Pavilion is silent; on the second floor the House Governor has his quarters in the old nurseries and schoolroom, but the ground and first floors are shut in the winter months and an unusual stillness reigns; a stillness, however, which is peaceful rather than oppressive: there are no ghosts at Osborne, yet there is an unmistakable air of graciousness in the whole building which convalescents find restful and reassuring, especially to the older generation, which cherishes these values.

# Epilogue

To see Osborne only as the home of Queen Victoria and her family is to miss its deeper significance as the focus, the rallying point of an entire dynasty. From those two plain but cluttered writing tables in the sitting-room letters, messages, demands and questions went out to every corner of Europe, wherever there might be found a member of the Queen's vast family. She and Prince Albert were the founders of a complex but short-lived dynasty: it was to end abruptly with the first shells fired in the Great War. Victoria and Albert symbolised Imperial progress in a spirit of wealth, confidence and security. Osborne, especially when seen from the sea, reflects that security: it stands four-square, massive, complete and – it must be admitted – majestic. This is the paradox of Osborne – a great house built to serve a Queen and Empress but which contrived, somehow, to impart serenity to a small figure who, in her 'ordinariness', despite blows of bereavement and misfortune, continued to care for her people, and could weep for them in their sorrows.

# Appendix: The Royal Yachts

The Queen was a great traveller. She made numerous journeys to the continent, almost invariably crossing the Channel in one or other of the Royal Yachts. Her visits to the West Country and to Ireland were also made in these ships; on the former she could sail down the coast from port to port according to the arrangements, and there was the undoubted advantage in not having to make elaborate preparations for a stay ashore, not only for herself, but for her maids and the whole suite in attendance. Not that this would have made much difference to the Queen, perhaps; she was not always considerate in her dealings with the Household. The Queen's use of Osborne, too, brought into use a fleet of yachts and auxiliaries with visitors, correspondence and messengers. In 1849, soon after the Queen took up residence at Osborne, the *Elfin*, a steam yacht for Isle of Wight service, ran the following routine:

> 10.0 a.m. left Portsmouth Harbour with London papers and official correspondence for Osborne, landing them at Osborne Bay, thence proceeding to Cowes. 2.0 p.m. leave Cowes with Queen's Messenger for Southampton, and there embark another for Cowes. Leave Cowes at 7.0 a.m. for Portsmouth.

Occasions of state or national emergency could double the work of the auxiliaries. The jetty at Osborne Bay was not much used but Trinity Pier at East Cowes was the familiar point for the yachts to berth. On state occasions the pier would be decorated with flags and bunting, and it was a common sight to observe members of the Royal family being greeted on arrival, or themselves greeting their visitors.

The Queen seems to have enjoyed her sea trips but, in contrast to travelling on land, she always liked her yachts to steam as fast

153

as possible. In the first *Victoria and Albert*, a paddle steamer, she made a voyage to Le Tréport in company with Lady Bloomfield, one of her Ladies, who wrote:

> I remained on deck a long time with Her Majesty, and she taught me to plait paper for bonnets, which was a favourite occupation of the Queen's. Lady Canning and I had settled ourselves in a very sheltered place protected by the paddle-box. . . . Her Majesty sent for her camp-stool and settled herself between us, plaiting away most composedly, when suddenly we observed a commotion among the sailors; little knots of men talking together in a mysterious manner. The Queen was much puzzled and asked what was the matter, and inquired whether we were going to have a mutiny on board. . . . Lord Adolphus laughed but remarked that he really did not know what would happen unless Her Majesty would be graciously pleased to move her seat. 'Your Majesty is unwittingly closing up the door of the place where the grog tubs are kept and so the men cannot have their grog.' 'Oh, very well,' said the Queen, 'on one condition, namely that you bring me a glass of grog.' This was accordingly done, and after tasting it the Queen said, 'I am afraid that I can only make the same remark that I did once before, that I think it would be very good if it were stronger.'[2]

In 1855 the *Victoria and Albert II* was brought into service, the old ship being renamed the *Osborne*. The Queen's apartments were comfortably furnished in mahogany, with chintz coverings. Green silk blinds covered the windows, with curtains of white muslin with goffered frills. The new *Victoria and Albert* was, like her forbear, a paddle steamer, capable of some 15 knots, and with two yellow funnels. It was on board the *Alberta*, a smaller vessel which the Queen often used to carry her between Portsmouth and the Isle of Wight, that a tragedy occurred in 1875. She was involved in a collision with the schooner *Mistletoe* which, under sail, had gone about unexpectedly. The Queen was distressed and delayed her departure from Portsmouth until she had learned the details. Three men were killed in the collision, and at the subsequent inquiry there was some doubt cast, not only on the speed the *Alberta* was doing at the time, but also on the propriety of such a speed.

A typical trip for the *Alberta* may be noted when, in 1882, the Queen sailed in her across Spithead to Stokes Bay, where she visited Haslar Naval Hospital to visit the wounded and bestow decorations on some of the men for their service during the Egyptian campaign.

# List of Works Consulted

*(The abbreviated form of Sources shown in the Reference Section is given in brackets.)*

*A Family Album*, H.R.H. The Duke of Windsor, Cassell & Co., 1960

*A King's Story*, H.R.H. The Duke of Windsor, Cassell & Co., 1951

*Albert & Victoria*, David Duff, Frederick Muller, 1972

*Correspondence of Sarah Spencer, Lady Lyttelton*, Ed. Mrs. Wyndham, (Lyttelton), John Murray, 1912

*Daughters of Queen Victoria*, E. F. Benson, Cassell & Co., 1939

*Dear and Honoured Lady*, Hope Dyson & Charles Tennyson, (Dear and Honoured Lady), Macmillan, 1969

*Dearest Child*, Roger Fulford (Ed.) (Dearest Child), Evans Bros., 1964

*Dearest Mama*, Roger Fulford (Ed.) (Dearest Mama), Evans Bros., 1968

*Edward VII and His Circle*, Virginia Cowles, Hamish Hamilton, 1956

*The Greville Memoirs*, Longmans, Green & Co., 1875–87

*Henry Ponsonby: His Life from His Letters* (Ponsonby), Arthur Ponsonby, Macmillan, 1942

*King Edward VII*, Vol I, Sidney Lee, Macmillan, 1925

*King Edward VII*, Philip Magnus, John Murray, 1964

*Edward VII*, Christopher Hibbert, Allen Lane, 1976

*King George V*, Harold Nicolson, Constable, 1952

*Lady Lytton's Court Diary*, Mary Lutyens (Ed.), Rupert Hart-Davis, 1961

*The Letters of Queen Victoria*, First Series, Ed. A. C. Benson & Viscount Esher, Second Series, Ed. G. E. Buckle, Third Series, Ed. G. E. Buckle, (Letters), John Murray, 1907, 1926, 1930

156

*Further Letters of Queen Victoria*, (Further Letters), (Ed. Hector Bolitho), Thornton Butterworth, 1938

*Letters of the Prince Consort*, (Jagow) Ed. Kurt Jagow trans. Dugdale, John Murray, 1938

*Life of the Prince Consort*, (Martin) Theodore Martin, 5 Volumes, Smith Elder & Co., 1875–80

*Life with Queen Victoria*, (Mallet) Victor Mallet, John Murray, 1968

*The Mountbattens*, Alden Hatch, W. H. Allen, 1966

*My Memories of Six Reigns*, H.H. Princess Marie Louise, Evans Bros., 1956

*Princes in the Making*, Morris Marples, Faber & Faber, 1965

*Princess Alice*, H.R.H. Princess Christian, John Murray, 1884

*Queen Alexandra*, Mrs. C. N. Williamson, Partridge & Co., 1902

*A Queen at Home*, Vera Watson, W. H. Allen, 1952

*Queen Mary*, (Queen Mary) J. Pope-Hennessy, George Allen & Unwin, 1959

*The Queen Thanks Sir Howard*, (McClintock), Mary McClintock, John Murray, 1945

*Queen Victoria*, E. F. Benson, Longmans, 1935

*Queen Victoria*, Helmut and Alison Gernsheim, Longmans, 1959

*Queen Victoria*, Lytton Strachey, Chatto & Windus, 1949

*Queen Victoria: Her Life and Times*, (Life and Times) Cecil Woodham-Smith, Hamish Hamilton, 1972

*Queen Victoria's Mother*, Dulcie M. Ashdown, Robert Hale, 1974

*Queen Victoria's Private Life*, E. E. P. Tisdall, Jarrolds, 1961

*Reminiscences of Court and Diplomatic Life*, Vol. I, Georgiana, Baroness Bloomfield, Kegan Paul, Trench, 1883

*Recollections of Three Reigns*, Frederick Ponsonby; Eyre, Spottiswoode, 1957

*Royal Progress*, Hector Bolitho, Batsford, 1937

*The Empress Brown*, Tom Cullen, Bodley Head 1969

*The Royal Yachts*, G. M. Gavin, Rich & Cowan, 1932

*The Shy Princess*, David Duff, Evans Bros., 1958

*Thomas Cubitt, Master Builder*, (Hobhouse), Hermione Hobhouse, Macmillan, 1971

*Twenty Years at Court*, Hon. Eleanor Stanley, Nisbet & Co., 1916

*Vicky* (Vicky), Daphne Bennett, Collins & Harvill Press, 1971

*Victoria R.I.*, (Longford), Elizabeth Longford, Weidenfeld & Nicolson, 1964

*Victoria Travels*, David Duff, Frederick Muller, 1970

*Your Dear Letter*, Ed. Roger Fulford, Evans Bros., 1971

*The Illustrated London News*

*The Times*

*The Osborne Magazine*

*Isle of Wight County Press*

# References

*(Sources given in brackets may be found in the List of Works Consulted.)*

Page 5 Queen Victoria to the Princess Royal, as dated. (Dearest Child)

1. *Beginnings*
   1  *The Illustrated London News*, March 16, 1844
   2  Queen Victoria, *Journal*, Oct. 19, 1843 (Longford)
   3  Ibid. Oct. 15, 1844 (Hobhouse)
   4  Prince Albert to Sir Robert Peel, Oct. 21, 1844 (Hobhouse)
   5  Ibid.
   6  *The Illustrated London News*, March 16, 1844
   6a *Life and Times*, p. 274 (Cecil Woodham Smith)
   7  Mr. Anson to Mr. Edward White, Jan. 17, 1845 (Hobhouse)
   8  Queen Victoria to the King of the Belgians, Mar. 25, 1845 (Letters I, Vol ii)
   9  Queen Victoria, *Journal*, May 17, 1845 (Hobhouse)
   10 *The Illustrated London News*, May 17, 1845
   11 Queen Victoria, *Journal*, June 23, 1845 (Hobhouse)
   12 Ibid. March 1, 1846 (Hobhouse)
   13 Charles Greville, *Memoirs*. Vol V
   14 Lady Lyttelton, *Correspondence*. p. 364
   15 Ibid. p. 361
   16 Ibid. p. 361
   17 Ibid. p. 358
   18 Hon. Eleanor Stanley, Letters, as dated (*Twenty Years at Court*)
   19 Ibid. 18 July, 1856 (*Twenty Years at Court*)
   20 Ibid. 14 July, 1860 (*Twenty Years at Court*)
   21 Ibid. 3 March, 1861 (*Twenty Years at Court*)

2. *Prince Albert*
   1  Prince Albert to the Princess Royal, as dated. (Martin)
   2  Prince Albert to Baron Stockmar, August 16, 1853 (Martin)

3   Prince Albert to Queen Victoria, undated, April, 1859 (Life and Times)
4   Prince Albert to the Princess Royal, May 18, 1859 (Martin)
5   Prince Albert to Baron Stockmar, December 8, 1859 (Martin)
6   Prince Albert to the Princess Royal, December, 1859 (Martin)
7   Ibid. (Martin)

3. *The Children of Osborne*
1   Queen Victoria to Queen Augusta of Prussia, Oct. 6, 1856 (*The Shy Princess*)
2   Lady Lyttelton, *Correspondence*, August 18, 1846
3   Diaries of Frederick W. Gibbs (*Cornhill Magazine*)
4   Queen Victoria, *Journal*, Aug. 8, 1845 (Victoria Travels, p. 77)
5   Queen Victoria to the Princess Royal, May 26, 1858 (Dearest Child)
6   Ibid. May 29, 1858 (Dearest Child)
7   Queen Victoria, *Journal*, Aug. 6, 1858 (Martin)
8   Ibid. Aug. 31, 1858 (Martin)

4. *Court Life*
1   Queen Victoria to Sir Henry Ponsonby, as dated. (Ponsonby, p. 117)
2   *Life with Queen Victoria*, p. 12, (Mallet)
3   Ibid. p. 13, (Mallet)
4   Ibid. p. 14, (Mallet)

6. *'Day turned into Night'*
1   Queen Victoria to the Princess Royal, Feb. 3, 1858, (Jagow)
2   Prince Albert to the Princess Royal, Feb. 3, 1858, (Jagow)
3   Queen Victoria, *Journal*, Feb. 2, 1858 (Martin)
4   Prince Albert to Baron Stockmar, Nov. 14, 1861 (Martin)
5   Martin, Vol V, p. 411
6   Queen Victoria, *Journal*, Nov. 14, 1861
7   Prince Albert to Queen Victoria, quoted Martin, Vol. V, p. 415.
8   Disraeli, Mem. 1862

7. *A Widow's Seclusion*
1   Queen Victoria to the King of the Belgians, Dec. 20, 1861 (*Letters I*, iii)
2   Ibid. as dated (*Letters I*, iii)
3   Queen Victoria to Sir Theodore Martin, 1863, quoted Martin, Vol V.
4   from 'Twenty Years at Court' (Stanley)
5   Ibid. (Stanley)
6   Princess Royal to Queen Victoria, Feb. 17, 1861 ('Vicky') p. 114

8. *Princess Alexandra at Osborne*
    1   Queen Victoria to the Princess Royal, November 6, 1862 (*Dearest Mama*, p. 125)
    2   Ibid. November 8, 1862 (Ibid. p. 127)

9. *John Brown*
    1   Queen Victoria to the Princess Royal, April 5, 1865 (*Your Dear Letter*, pp. 21–2)
    2   '*The Empress Brown*', p. 183.
    3   Queen Victoria to Sir Henry Ponsonby, March, 1883, (Ponsonby, p. 129)
    4   Sir Henry Ponsonby to Lady Ponsonby, April, 1883, (Ibid. p. 128)

10. *The Prince of Wales at Osborne*
    1   Queen Victoria to Princess Royal, 14 February, 1972, (Magnus)

11. *Visitors*
    1   Visit to Osborne, April 14, 1862, (*Dear and Honoured Lady*, pp. 69–70)
    2   Diary of Emily Tennyson, May 9, 1862 (Ibid. pp. 75–6)
    3   Queen Victoria, Journal, August 7, 1883 (Ibid. pp. 102–3)

12. *1878 – An Eventful Year*
    1   Queen Victoria, *Journal*, as dated
    2   Grand Duchess of Hesse to Queen Victoria, November 16, 1878 – telegram (Princess Alice, p. 369)

13. *The Wedding of Princess Beatrice*
    1   Queen Victoria to Duke of Grafton, *Letters II*, iii, p. 593)
    2   *The Illustrated London News*, August 1885
    3   Queen Victoria to the Princess Royal, January 7, 1885, (Longford)
    4   Queen Victoria, *Journal*, July 23, 1885 (*The Shy Princess* p. 185)

14. *Queen Victoria and the Munshi*
    1   Duke of York to King Edward VII, December, 1905 (Nicolson)
    2   from *Life with Queen Victoria*, (Mallet), p. 172

15. *Princess May at Osborne*
    1   Queen Victoria to the Empress of Prussia, February 13, 1892 (*Queen Mary*, p. 128)
    2   Queen Victoria to the Duke of York, May, 1893, (Nicolson)
    3   Queen Victoria to the Empress of Prussia, August 5, 1893 (*Queen Mary*, p. 284)

4   Duchess of York to the Duchess of Teck, August 3, 1893, (Ibid.
    p. 284)
6   Duchess of York to the Duchess of Teck, August 3, 1893, (Ibid.
    p. 286)
7   Ibid.

16. *Death of Prince Henry*
1   Princess Marie Louise, *My Memories of Six Reigns*, Ch. 5.
2   from *Life with Queen Victoria*, (Mallet), p. 131
3   Ibid.
4   Duchess of York to Prince Adolphus of Teck, January 28, 1896
    (*Queen Mary*, p. 317)

17. *Queen Victoria at Work*
1   Sir Francis Knollys to Sir Henry Ponsonby, note, December,
    1891
2   Lady Lytton, 'Court Diary' 1899, as dated.

18. *Last Years*
1   Queen Victoria, *Journal*, as dated (Longford)
2   Diagnosis of the Queen Victoria's last Illness. (Isle of Wight
    County Press)

19. *The Queen's Death at Osborne*
1   Queen Victoria, *Journal*, as dated (Longford, et al.)
2   Ibid.
3   Ibid.
4   *Recollections of Three Reigns*
5   Ibid.
6   Duchess of York, Diary, January 22, 1901 (*Queen Mary* p. 353)

20. *Queen Victoria's Departure from Osborne*
1   Duchess of York to the Grand Duchess of Mecklenburg-Strelitz,
    January 17, 1901 (*Queen Mary* p. 353)

21. *Royal Naval College, Osborne*
1   Duchess of York to Duke of York, December 12, 1901 (*Queen
    Mary*, p. 356)
2   King Edward VII to A. J. Balfour, August 9, 1902 (*The Times*)
3   *The Illustrated London News*, 1903
4   Duke of Windsor, *A King's Story*, Ch. IV
5   Prince Louis of Battenberg to Princess Louise of Battenberg,
    October 19, 1913 (Broadlands Archives)
6   *The Osborne Magazine*, December, 1905
7   Public Record Office, ADM 116/1185A

# Index

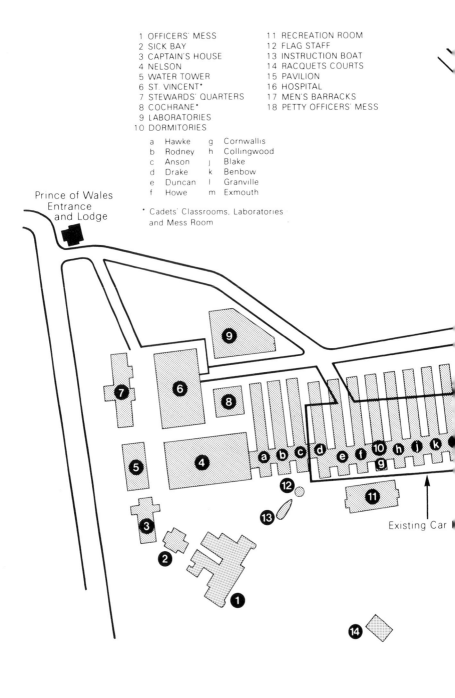

1 OFFICERS' MESS
2 SICK BAY
3 CAPTAIN'S HOUSE
4 NELSON
5 WATER TOWER
6 ST. VINCENT*
7 STEWARDS' QUARTERS
8 COCHRANE*
9 LABORATORIES
10 DORMITORIES

11 RECREATION ROOM
12 FLAG STAFF
13 INSTRUCTION BOAT
14 RACQUETS COURTS
15 PAVILION
16 HOSPITAL
17 MEN'S BARRACKS
18 PETTY OFFICERS' MESS

a   Hawke        g   Cornwallis
b   Rodney       h   Collingwood
c   Anson        j   Blake
d   Drake        k   Benbow
e   Duncan       l   Granville
f   Howe         m   Exmouth

* Cadets' Classrooms, Laboratories
  and Mess Room

Prince of Wales
Entrance
and Lodge

Existing Car

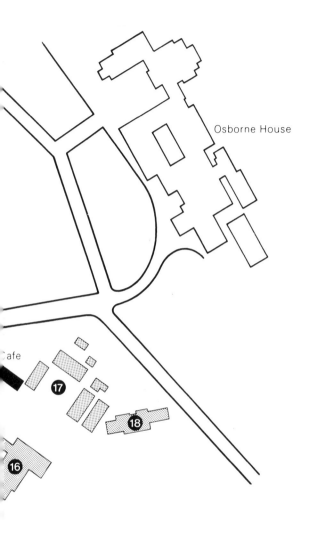

Osborne House

afe

Plan of Royal Naval College 1903–1921